MW01232711

Winning Life's Race:
Seven Keys To Victory

By

Robert F. Litro, Ph.D.

Kendall – my brother in Christ,
may your "Life's Race" bring
you peace and glorify God

Bob

4/29/09

ISBN 0-7414-1158-x

Scriptures taken from the New King James Version.
©1979,1980, 1982 by Thomas Nelson, Inc.
Used by permission. All rights reserved.

Published by:

519 West Lancaster Avenue
Haverford, PA 19041-1413
Info@buybooksontheweb.com
www.buybooksontheweb.com
Toll-free (877) BUY BOOK
Local Phone (610) 520-2500
Fax (610) 519-0261

Printed in the United States of America

Printed on Recycled Paper

Published June, 2002

Dedication

For my dear parents, Louise and Albert Litro,
and sister, Alberta Litro Cannonier
Their examples helped form my standards.

To my loving wife, Jane, in believing in me,
you have added strength to my life.

To my Lord and Savior, Jesus Christ,
who said,
*I am the way, the truth, and the life. No
one comes to the Father except through Me.*
John 14:6

Table of Contents

Preface   iii

Introduction   iv

Chapter 1   Character   1

Chapter 2   Integrity   22

Chapter 3   Courage   46

Chapter 4   Attitude   67

Chapter 5   Habit   85

Chapter 6   Goals   107

Chapter 7   Faith   122

Preface

Against the tragic backdrop of world events today, the collection of quotations, Bible verses, and brief stories, that make up *Winning Life's Race: Seven Keys To Victory*, may appear quite unimportant. Nevertheless, since the beginning of American freedom, faith and trust in the supreme power of God to direct men's lives, has always been America's own creed.

Since America today is defending what is her own birthright as a free nation, under God, this collection of quotations, Bible verses, and brief stories form an important part of what the country now is fighting to save. Americans, as never before, are as aware of human values present as they are against an evil conception of a world devoid of such values.

Winning Life's Race: Seven Keys To Victory reflects the renewed recognition of the need for certain fundamental human characteristics, without which no nation can survive as a civilized state. These characteristics are; character, integrity, courage, attitude, habits, goals, and faith.

These pages include quotations, Bible verses, and memo stories I have found to be inspiring, encouraging, and strengthening my resolve to win life's race, claiming the prize as a follower of Jesus Christ.

I hope you will agree that this is the only life's race worth running.

Note: The material contained in this book was collected over a period of years from a variety of sources, including God's Word, the Bible, the most important source of all.

Authors of many quotations are unknown and some of the sayings have been attributed to more than one author. Therefore, it is often impossible to list each author

Winning Life's Race: Seven Keys To Victory

Introduction

"Winning Life's Race: Seven Keys To Victory" is an collection of inspirational quotes, stories, and Scriptures encouraging us to make meaningful, productive, and joyful life decisions. Basic, practical and filled with the timeless wisdom of the Bible, as well as man's insights, *Winning Life's Race* offers a road map for victory in life's daily journey.

"..........let us run with endurance the race that is set before us, looking unto Jesus the author and finisher of our faith; who for the joy that was set before him endured the cross, despising the shame, and has sat down at the right hand of the throne of God. Hebrews 12:1-3

"Winning Life's Race" places seven words in our "mental bank account." They are: Character, Integrity, Courage, Attitude, Habits, Goals, and Faith.

These worthy words bring life, stamina, and strength to our being. These words influence our life, our hearts, and ultimately, our actions. In times of need, we can draw strength from this "mental bank account", and meet the challenges of life's race with hope, faith, and trust.

To "win" life's race, however, we must continually commit ourselves to discover, rediscover and implant in our lives, the core ingredients of these seven key words. In this journey, self-honesty must be our constant companion. Wealth can be inherited, but wisdom has to be learned.

Winning Life's Race is based on the belief expressed in Romans 8:28:*And we know that all things work together for good to those who love God, to those who are the called according to His purpose.*

The book has three purposes. The first purpose is to provide thoughts and stories inspiring us to run life's daily race with the fuel of hope, trust, and faith that the Bible provides. The second purpose is to present thoughts and stories to smile about, be encouraged by, and rejoice about. The final goal is to develop within each of us the personal commitment and sacrifice necessary for *"Winning Life's Race."*

A fundamental value defining America is: "One nation, under God". Without commitment to this value, the terms, humanity, America, and community become empty words.

Success in dealing with this fundamental value will not come from *mental detectors*, such as the SAT [Scholastic Achievement Tests]; or *metal detectors*, such as used in airport, public buildings, and schools. What is needed are *moral detectors* that will ring loud and clear the message of core values.

In Ecclesiastes 12:13, we find our instruction: *"..fear God and keep His commandments. For this is man's all."* To fear God means to revere, worship, and serve God - to turn from evil and turn in awe to the living God. It does <u>not</u> involve dread, but instead a proper respect for and obedience to our Creator.

There is a "life's race" for each of us. *For I know the thoughts I have toward you, thoughts of peace and not of evil, to give you a future and a hope.* Jeremiah 29:11

As you read *"Winning Life's Race"*, allow God's words, the quotations, and stories, to strengthen you. You may well discover as you deal with your deepest longings, thoughts, hurts, and prayers, how much God's message is already a part of your innermost being..

Our American spirit of democracy: "One nation under God", has been passed on to us by generations that have gone before us. The legacy left to us, demands that we all promote those values that are worthy of our honor, trust, and respect.

Our prayer is that reading the right message at the right time in your life will reveal to you that *"Winning Life's Race"* comes from turning our hearts and heads over to the Holy Spirit so that the truths of God's Word can be manifested in our daily human existence.

We hope that this book will not only bless you as you read these quotes and stories, but that you will be a blessing to others by sharing the confident faith that Jesus Christ is the only way to salvation.

Chapter 1

Character

The word, **Character,** may be defined as follows: *the combination of qualities or features that distinguish one person, group, or thing from another. The stamp impressed by nature, education, or habit; that which a person or thing really is. Moral or ethical strength; integrity, fortitude; reputation.*

The word, **character,** comes from the Latin, [character] - mark, or distinctive quality, and, earlier, from the Greek word, [character] - to scratch or engrave.

Synonyms for character include: traits, nature, personality, disposition, individuality, and temperament.

Each of us has a character that is distinctly our own. Some people, however, may wish that they were someone different. Someone with different qualities or features. The Bible verses, quotations and stories in this chapter demonstrate that every individual makes daily choices and decisions. These choices combine to make up those qualities or features that distinguish us from other people.

A good name is rather to be chosen rather than great riches,
loving favor rather than silver and gold.
Proverbs 22:1
******

All scripture is given by inspiration of God, and is profitable for doctrine, for reproof, for correction, for instruction in righteousness, that the man of God may be complete, thoroughly equipped for every good work.
2nd Timothy 3:16-17.

1

Chapter 1   Character

The real test of character comes when doing
the right thing may not be in our self-interest.

Two Nickels and Five Pennies

When an ice cream sundae cost much less, a boy entered a coffee shop and sat at a table. A waitress put a glass of water in front of him. "How much is an ice cream sundae?"

"Fifty cents," replied the waitress.

The little boy pulled his hand out of his pocket and studied a number of coins in it. "How much is a dish of plain ice cream?" he inquired. Some people were now waiting for a table, and the waitress was impatient. "Thirty-five cents," she said angrily.

The little boy again counted the coins. "I'll have the plain ice cream."

The waitress brought the ice cream and walked away. The boy finished, paid the cashier, and departed. When the waitress came back, she swallowed hard at what she saw.

There, placed neatly beside the empty dish, were two nickels and five pennies--her tip.

Author Unknown

All that is necessary for evil to triumph
is for good people to do nothing.
Edmund Burke
******

We are on a journey to become more than
we think we are, and what God wants us to be.

Chapter 1   Character

Character is like a tree and reputation like
its shadow. The shadow is what we think of it;
the tree is the real thing.
Abraham Lincoln
******

Cowardice asks the question: is it safe?
Expediency asks the question: is it politic?
Vanity asks the question: is it popular?
But conscience asks the question: is it right?
And there comes a time when one must take a position
that is neither safe, nor politic, nor popular -
but one must take it because it is right.
Martin Luther King, Jr.
******

*No temptation has overtaken you except such as is common to man;
but God is faithful , who will not allow you to be tempted beyond
what you are able, but with the temptation will also make the way of
escape also, that you will be able to bear it.*
1st Corinthians 10:13:

While the spirit of neighborliness was important on the frontier
because neighbors were so few, it is even more important now because
our neighbors are so many.

Lady Bird Johnson

Every human being is intended to have a character
of his own; to be what no other is,
and to do what no other can do.
William Channing
******

Life is an uphill business for a guy who is not on the level.
John Welsh

Chapter 1   Character

A man who doesn't stand for something
will fall for anything.
Peter Marshall
******

Be sober spirit, be vigilant;. because your adversary, the devil, walks about like a roaring lion, seeking whom he may devour. Resist him, steadfast in faith, knowing that the same sufferings are experienced by your brotherhood in the world.
1st Peter 5:8-9:
******

People of character know the difference between
what they have a right to do, and what is right to do.
******

....He who is in you is greater than he who is in the world.
1st John 4:4b

The Six Mistakes of Man

Cicero, the Roman statesman and philosopher, wrote the following some 2,000 years ago

1. The delusion that personal gain is made by crushing others.
2. The tendency to worry about things that cannot be changed or corrected.
3. Insisting that a thing is impossible because we cannot accomplish it.
4. Refusing to set aside trivial preferences.
5. Neglecting development and refinement of the mind, and not acquiring the habit of reading and studying.
6. Attempting to compel others to believe and live as we do.

Chapter 1   Character

I would rather lose in a cause that I know
some day will triumph than to triumph
in a cause that I know some day will fail.
Wendell L. Wilkie
******

You never know how a horse will pull
until you hook him to a heavy load.
Paul "Bear" Bryant
******

Hard work spotlights the character of people: some turn up their
sleeves, some turn up their noses, and some don't turn up at all.
Sam Ewing

> When I was a young man, I wanted to change the world. I
> found it was difficult to change the world, so I tried to change my
> nation. When I found I couldn't change the nation, I began to focus on
> my town. I couldn't change the town and, as an older man, I tried to
> change my family.
>
> Now, as an old man, I realize the only thing I can change is
> myself, and suddenly I realize that if long ago I had changed myself, I
> could have made an impact on my family. My family and I could have
> made an impact on our town. Their impact could have changed the
> nation and I could indeed have changed the world.

If you don't have enemies, you don't have character.
Paul Newman
******

If we live in the Spirit, let us also walk in the Spirit.
Let us not become conceited, provoking
one another, envying one another.
Galatians 5:25-26

Chapter 1   Character

Character is not made in a crisis, it is only exhibited.
Robert Freeman
******

The measure of a man's character is what he would do
if he knew he never would be found out.
Baron Thomas Babington Macauley

The best index to a person's character is
(a) how he treats people who can't do him any good,
and
(b) how he treats people who can't fight back.
Abigail van Buren ("Dear Abby")

Every man has three characters:
that which he shows, that which he has,
and that which he thinks he has.
Alphonse Karr
******

You can easily judge the character of a man by how
he treats those who can do nothing for him.
Goethe
******

People of character do the right thing even
when it costs more than they want to pay
******

Whenever two people meet there are really six people present.
There is each man as he sees himself, each man as the other
person sees him, and each man as he really is.

Chapter 1   Character

> The story is told about a young father, not wanting to be bothered with his small son's questions, tore up a world map into small pieces, and told his son to put it back together --hoping that it would keep him busy while he read.
>
> Three minutes later the boy had the map put together. His dad wanted to know how in the world he did it.
>
> The boy said "There was a picture of a man on the other side, so I put the man together and by doing so, I put the world together. When I got the man together, the world was together." (If we get the small pieces in place, the larger ones will come together)

Character is not revealed by what we say,
or even what we intend; it is a reflection of what we do.
******

I am the light of the world. He who follows me
shall not walk in darkness but have the light of life.
John 8:12
******

The study of God's word, for the purpose of discovering God's will,
is the secret discipline which has formed the greatest characters.
J. W. Alexander
******

It is with trifles, and when he is off guard,
that a man best reveals his character.
Arthur Schopenhauer

> Wisdom, according to the early believers had a specific meaning. To those believers wisdom meant knowing the right thing to do and doing it.
>
> How do we find out what's right? The same way they did. They knew from Scripture.

7

Chapter 1   Character

The law of the Lord is perfect, converting the soul.
The testimony of the Lord is sure, making wise the simple.
Psalm 19:7
******

It has been observed that there is a downward
path in the progress of error.
The compromising believer:
> recognizes it
>> tolerates it
>>> excuses it
>>>> defends it
>>>>> condones it
>>>>>> embraces it

Life's Formula: The 3 R's

Respect - for ourselves and others

Responsibility - being accountable for our actions

Resourcefulness - learning to do the best with the gifts we
have been given

John Rosemond

The first and best victory is to conquer self; to be conquered by self
is, of all things, the most shameful and vile.
Plato

Chapter 1   Character

Perhaps at the Last Day all that will remain worth recording of a life
full of activity and zeal, will be those little deeds that were done
solely beneath the eye of God.

A Tale of Two 18th Century New Yorkers

A **legacy** is anything handed down from one generation to
another. Max Jukes, hostile to Christianity, kept his children away from
church.

Of his 1,026 descendants, 300 were sent to prison for terms
averaging 13 years; 190 were prostitutes; and 680 are known to have
been alcoholics.

Jonathan Edwards, his contemporary, was a powerful preacher
who helped lead America's Great Awakening revival in the 1700s. His
children grew up in the church.

His 929 descendants include 430 ministers, 86 university
professors, 13 university presidents, 75 authors, 7 U.S. Congressmen,
and one Vice-President.

An apology is a good way to have the last word!
******

*You are the salt of the earth but, if the salt loses its flavor, how shall
it be seasoned? It is then good for nothing but to be thrown out and
trampled underfoot by men.   You are the light of the world . A city
that is set on a hill cannot be hidden. .... Let your light so
shine before men, that they may see your good works, and glorify
your Father in Heaven.*
Matthew 5:13-14,16

Chapter 1   Character

How Rich Are You?

One day a father and his rich family took his young son on a trip to the country with the firm purpose to show him how poor people can be. They spent a day and a night on the farm of a very poor family. When they got back from their trip the father asked his son,

"How was the trip?" "Very good, Dad!"

"Did you see how poor people can be?" the father asked. "Yeah!"

"And what did you learn?"

The son answered, "I saw that we have a dog at home, and they have four. We have a pool that reaches to the middle of the garden, they have a creek that has no end. We have imported lamps in the garden, they have the stars. Our patio reaches to the front yard, they have a whole horizon."

When the little boy was finished, his father was speechless. His son added, "Thanks Dad for showing me how poor we are!"

Isn't it true that it all depends on the way you look at things? If you have love, friends, family, health, good humor and a positive attitude towards life - you've got everything! You can't buy any of these things. You can have all the material possessions you can imagine, provisions for the future, etc., but if you are poor of spirit, you have nothing!

Life's challenges are not supposed to paralyze you,
they're supposed to help you discover who you are.
Bernice Johnson Reagon
******

When you were born, you cried and the world rejoiced.
Live your life in such a manner that,
when you die, the world cries and you rejoice.
Native American Proverb

Chapter 1   Character

Do not lay not up for yourselves treasures on earth, where moth and rust destroy, and where thieves break in and steal; but lay up for yourselves treasures in heaven, where neither moth nor rust destroys and where thieves do not break in and steal.
Matthew 6:19-20
******

Let the honor of your neighbor be as dear to you as your own.
******

Whatever America hopes to bring to pass in the world must first come in the heart of America.
Dwight D. Eisenhower
******

If anyone desires to be first, he shall be last of all and servant of all..
Mark 9:35a

Jimmy Stewart gave his definition of a hero: Real heroes come in all shapes and sizes from all walks of life. But they have a few things in common:

- They are never so big that they can't bend down to help someone else.
- They are never so wise that they don't remember who taught them.
- They are never so strong that they can't be gentle.
- They are never so gifted that they won't share their skills with others.
- They are never so fearless that they don't play by the rules and live by the law.
- They are never such big winners that they forget what it feels like to lose.

Chapter 1   Character

It may make a difference to all eternity
whether we do right or wrong today.
James Freeman Clarke
******

Today is yesterday's pupil.
Benjamin Frankllin
******

There is always the battle to be fought before
the victory is won. Too many think they
must have the victory before the battle.
Dean Stanley
******

People are stained-glass windows. They sparkle and shine when the sun
is out, but when the darkness sets in,
their true beauty is revealed only if there is a light from within.
Elizabeth Kubler-Ross
******

I don't measure a man's success by how high he climbs
but how high he bounces when he hits bottom.
George S. Patton
******

*If my people, who are called by My name, will humble themselves, and
pray, and seek My face, and turn from their wicked ways; then will I
hear from heaven, and will forgive their sin, and heal their land.*
2nd Chronicles 7:14

Chapter 1   Character

Our background and circumstances may have influenced who we are, but we are responsible for who we become.
James Rhinehart

> After the cheers have died down and the stadium is empty, after the headlines have been written and after you are back in the quiet of your room and the championship ring has been placed on the dresser and all the pomp and fanfare has faded, the enduring things that are left are: the dedication to excellence, the dedication to victory, and the dedication to doing with our lives the very best we can to make the world a better place in which to live.
> Vince Lombardi

If someone says, 'I love, God,' and hates his brother,
he is a liar; for he who does not love his brother
whom he has seen, how can he love God whom he has not seen?
1 John 4:20
******

We lie loudest when we lie to ourselves.
Eric Hoffer
******

The people of every country are the only guardians of their own rights, and are the only instruments which can be used for their destruction.
Thomas Jefferson
******

But the fruit of the Spirit is love, joy, peace, longsuffering,
kindness, goodness, faithfulness, gentleness,
self-control. Against such there is no law.
Galatians 5:22-23

13

Chapter 1   Character

To Risk

To laugh is to risk appearing the fool.

To weep is to risk appearing sentimental.

To reach out for another is to risk involvement.

To expose feelings is to risk exposing your true self.

To place your ideas, your dreams, before the crowd, is to risk loss.

To love is to risk not being loved in return.

To live is to risk dying.

To hope is to risk despair.

To try at all is to risk failure.

But risk we must.

Because the greatest hazard in life is to risk nothing.

Anonymous

Finally, brethren, whatever things are true, whatever things are noble, whatever things are just, whatever things are pure, whatever things are lovely, whatever things are of good report; if there is any virtue, and if there is anything praiseworthy, meditate on these things.
Philippians 4:8
******

The art of living lies not in eliminating,
but in growing with troubles.
Bernard M. Baruch
******

Character is what you are in the dark.
Unknown

Chapter 1   Character

I don't think you can legislate ethics. If we turn to the lawmakers for
everything, that will threaten our freedom
by shrinking it by making matters of moral choice
become matters of legal obligation.
Patricia Rainey Reese

The Upper Road
I'm going by the upper road,
For that still holds the sun;
I'm climbing through night's pastures
Where the starry rivers run;
If you should think to seek me
In my old dark abode,
You'll find this writing on the door:
"He's on the Upper Road."
Anonymous

Live your life so that your children can tell their children
that you not only stood for something wonderful - you acted on it.
Dan Zadra
******

You can outdistance that which is running after you,
but not what is running inside you.
Rwandan Proverb
******

Unless the Lord build the house,
they labor in vain that build it;
unless the Lord guards the city,
the watchman stays awake in vain.
Psalm 127:1

Chapter 1   Character

When you choose your friends, don't be short-changed
by choosing personality over character.
W. Somerset Maugham

******

And we know that all things work together for good

to those who love God, to those who

are the called according to His purpose.

Romans 8:28

******

Do not think that what your thoughts dwell upon

is of no matter. Your thoughts are making you.

Bishop Steere

We learn wisdom from failure much more than from success.

We often discover what will do by finding out what will not do;

and probably he who never made a mistake never made a discovery.

Samuel Smiles

The man of worth is really great without being proud;

the mean man is proud without being really great.

Chinese Proverb

******

No person was ever honored for what he received.

Honor has been the reward for what he gave.

Calvin Coolidge

16

Chapter 1   Character

Behold the proud, his soul is not upright in him;
but the just shall live by his faith.
Habakkuk 2:4
******

Don't worry about opposition. Remember,
a kite rises against the wind, not with the wind.
Hamilton Wright Mabie
******

A long habit of not thinking a thing wrong
gives it a superficial appearance of being right.
Thomas Paine
******

An whatever you do in word or deed, do all in the name
of the Lord Jesus, giving thanks to God the Father through Him.
Colossians 3:17
******

You have not converted a man because you have silenced him.
John, Viscount Morley
******

A man cannot be comfortable without his own approval.
Mark Twain

Chapter 1   Character

Commit your works to the Lord, and
your thoughts will be established.
Proverbs 16:3
******

Our voluntary thoughts not only reveal what we are,
they predict what we will become.
A.W. Tozer
******

Lord, send me where Thou wilt, only go with me;
lay on me what Thou wilt, only sustain me.
Cut any cord but the one that binds me to Thy cause, to Thy heart.
Titus Coan
******

We cannot inherit Christianity. We might have had Christian
fathers and mothers, but that situation did not necessarily
produce Christian children. God has no grandchildren.
Billy Graham

Chapter 1   Character

The Statue

After World War II, German students volunteered to help rebuild a cathedral in England, one of many casualties of the Luftwaffe bombings. As the work progressed, debate broke out on how to best restore the large statue of Jesus with His arms outstretched and bearing the familiar inscription, "Come unto Me."

Careful patching could repair all damage to the statue except for Christ's hands, which had been destroyed by bomb fragments. Should they attempt the delicate task of reshaping those hands?

Finally the workers reached a decision that still stands today. The statue of Jesus has no hands, and the inscription now reads, *"Christ has no hands but ours."*

Dr. Paul Brand and Philip Yancy, from *Fearfully and Wonderfully Made.*

On God for all events depend. You cannot want when God's your friend. Weigh well your part and do your best. Leave to your Maker all the rest.

Matthew Cotton

******

After counting your blessings, ask God to show you how to multiply them by dividing them.

Lucien E. Coleman, Jr

Chapter 1   Character

We can learn something from bank tellers about how to determine what is true and what is false. Banks train their tellers to recognize counterfeit bills by making them memorize the characteristics of the legitimate paper monies.

If bank tellers were to set out to memorize all the different traits of counterfeit bills, they would never complete the task and would become confused in the process.

By learning the traits of the genuine, they prepare to recognize the false when it appears.

I am not what I ought to be,

I am not what I wish to be,

I am not even what I hope to be.

But, by God's Grace and Christ's love,

I am not what I was.

******

Many a man's reputation would not know

his character if they met on the street.
Elbert Hubbard

******

Where your treasure is, there your heart will be also.

Matthew 6:21

Chapter 1   Character

Jesus resisted the devil in His humanity. He did so with
Scripture, prayer, total dedication to God's will, and the
power of the Holy Spirit. All these are available to us.

Herschel Hobbs

******

*As each one has received a gift; minister to one another, as good
stewards of the manifold grace of God. If anyone speaks, let him speak
as the oracles of God. If anyone ministers, let him do it as with the
ability which God supplies, that in all things God may be glorified
through Jesus Christ, to whom belong the glory and the dominion
forever and ever. Amen.*

1 Peter 4:10-11

Chapter 2

Integrity

The word, **Integrity**, has these meanings: *the quality or condition of being whole or undivided; moral soundness especially as it is revealed in dealings that test steadfastness to truth, purpose, responsibility, or trust. Rigid adherence to a code of behavior.* The word, **integrity**, derives from the Latin, integritas, meaning. whole, or entire.

Synonyms for integrity include: soundness, completeness, reliability, standards, honesty, sincerity, dignity, and incorruptibility.

The possession of integrity comes from having God's word as a guide providing instructions for doing the right things. His Word provides us with hope and help to acquire wisdom through truth that overcomes the world's pull.

Having integrity means that we seek to live a life that faithfully submits to God's will as set forth in the Bible, and avoiding the worldly mentality that says: "When in Rome, do as the Romans do".

Be diligent to present yourself approved to God,

a worker who does not need to be ashamed,

rightly dividing the Word of Truth.

2nd Timothy 2:15

Chapter 2   Integrity

He has shown you, O man, what is good; and what does the Lord require of you but to do justly, to love mercy, and to walk humbly with your God?

Micah 6:8

******

The highest reward for a person's toil

is not what they get for it, but what they become by it.

John Ruskin

These are the times that try men's souls. The summer soldier and the sunshine patriot will, in this crisis, shrink from the service of their country; but he that stands it *now*, deserves the love and thanks of men and women.

Thomas Paine

I know not what course others may take,

but as for me, give me liberty or give me death.

Patrick Henry

******

A good test for a conversation: if you wouldn't

write it down and sign you name to it, don't say it.

Chapter 2   Integrity

Do not labor for the food which perishes, but for the food

which endures to everlasting life, which the Son of Man will give you....

John 6:27a-b

Those who preserve their integrity remain unshaken by the storms of daily life. They do not stir like leaves on a tree or follow the herd where it runs. In their mind remains the ideal attitude and conduct of living. This is not something given to them by others. It is their roots ... it is a strength that exists deep within them.

Native American Saying

We make a living by what we get;

we make a life by what we give.

W.A. Nance

******

Nearly all men can stand adversity,

but if you want to test a man's character, give him power.
Abraham Lincoln

******

Conviction is worthless unless it is converted into conduct.

Thomas Carlyle

Chapter 2   Integrity

We Need People
...who cannot be bought
...whose word is their bond
...who put character above wealth
...who possess opinions and a will
... who are larger than their vocations
...who do not hesitate to take chances
...who will make no compromise with wrong
...who will not lose their individuality in a crowd
...who will be as honest in small things as in great things
...who will not say they do it "because everybody else does it."
...whose ambitions are not confined to their own selfish desires
...who give thirty-six inches to the yard
...who will not have one brand of honesty for business purposes and
        another for private life
...who are true to their friends through good rapport and bad rapport, in
        adversity as well as in prosperity
...who do not believe that shrewdness, sharpness, and cunning, are the best
        qualities for winning success
...who are not ashamed or afraid to stand for the truth when it is unpopular
...who can say 'no' with emphasis, although the rest of the world says 'yes'

For the Lord does not see as man sees;
for man looks at the outward appearance,
but the Lord looks at the heart.
1 Samuel 16:7b

Chapter 2   Integrity

One ought never to turn one's back on a threatened danger and try to run away from it. If you do that, you will double the danger. But if you meet it promptly and without flinching you will reduce the danger by half.
Sir Winston Churchill

There is no pillow so soft as a clear conscience.
French proverb

If you treat people as they are, they will stay as they are. But if you treat them as if they were what they ought to be, and could be, they will become what they ought to be, and could be.
Goethe

Your word I have hidden in my heart
that I might not sin against You.
Psalm 119:11
******

There is no right way to do the wrong thing.
******

Laws control the lesser man ...
right conduct controls the greater one.
Mark Twain

Chapter 2   Integrity

*If any of you lacks wisdom, let him ask of God, who gives to all
liberally and without reproach, and it will be given to him.*
James 1:5
******
When I want to speak, let me first think: Is it true?
Is it kind? Is it necessary? If not, let it be left unsaid.

God Measures Greatness By Service

During the American Revolution, a noncommissioned officer was directing the repairs of a military building. He was barking orders to the soldiers under his command, trying to get them to raise a heavy wooden beam.

As the men struggled in vain to life the beam into place, a man who was passing by stopped to ask the one in charge why he wasn't helping the men. With all the pomp of an emperor, the soldier responded, "Sir, I am a corporal!"

"You are, are you?" replied the passerby,"I was not aware of that." Then, taking off his hat and bowing, he said, "I ask your pardon, Corporal." Then the stranger walked over and strained with the soldiers to lift the heavy beam.

After the job was finished, he turned and said, "Mr. Corporal, when you have another such job, and have not enough men send for your Commander in Chief, and I will come and help you a second time."

The corporal was thunderstruck. The person speaking to him was General Washington.

---

*I am the light of the world. He who follows Me
shall not walk in darkness but have the light of life.*
John 8:12 a-b

Chapter 2   Integrity

Delight yourself also in the Lord, and He shall give you the desires of your heart. Commit your way to the Lord, Trust also in Him, and He shall bring it to pass.
Psalm 37:4-5

It was an old English clergyman who suggested an apt comparison between the Bible and a sundial.

He said that a person could well read the figures on a dial, but would obviously know nothing of the exact hour unless the sun was shining on it.

Similarly, he suggested, a person could read the Bible through, but unless the Spirit of God was permitted to enlighten the Word, it was just a compilation of lofty but abstract ideas.

The law of the Lord is perfect, converting the soul.
The testimony of the Lord is sure, making wise the simple.
Psalm 19:7.
******

There is nothing wrong with men possessing riches.
The wrong comes when riches possess men.
Billy Graham
******

It is better to know some of the questions than all of the answers.
James Thurber
******

Getting me into hot water is often
God's way of keeping me clean.

Finders, Keepers...or Givers?

A wise woman who was traveling in the mountains found a precious stone in a stream. The next day she met another traveler who was hungry, and the wise woman opened her bag to share her food. The hungry traveler saw the precious stone and asked the woman to give it to him. She did so without hesitation.

The traveler left, rejoicing in his good fortune. He knew the stone was worth enough to give him security for a lifetime. But a few days later he came back to return the stone to the wise woman. "I've been thinking," he said, "I know how valuable the stone is, but I give it back in the hope that you can give me something even more precious:

Give me what you have within you that enabled you to give me the stone."

Let us be givers just as God is a giver. He loves us so much that He gave His only begotten Son, Our Lord Jesus Christ. If God did that for us then the least we could do is love others and share His love by caring and doing for others as He has done for us.

Colossians 3:17, *And whatever you do in word or deed, do all in the name of the Lord Jesus, giving thanks to God the Father through Him.*

Colossians 3:23-24, *"Whatever you do, do it heartily, as to the Lord and not to men ,knowing that from the Lord you will receive the reward of inheritance; for you serve the Lord Christ.*

I am not bound to win, but I am bound to be true. I am not bound to succeed, but I am bound to live up to what light I have.

Chapter 2   Integrity

I must stand with anybody that stands right; stand with him while
he is right and part with him when he goes wrong.
Abraham Lincoln
******

Give me, Lord, eyes to behold the truth; a seeing sense that knows the
eternal right; a heart with pity filled, and gentlest truth; a manly faith that
makes all darkness light.
Theodore Parker
******

*....unless a grain of wheat falls into the ground and dies, it remains
alone; but if it dies, it produces much grain.*
John 12:24a

The supreme test of goodness is not in the greater but in the
smaller incidents of our character and practice; not what we are when
standing in the searchlight of public scrutiny, but when we reach the
firelight flicker of our homes; not what we are when some clarion-call rings
thought he air, summoning us to fight for life and liberty, but our attitude
when we are called to sentry-duty in the grey morning, when the watch-fire
is burning low.

It is impossible to be our best at the supreme moment if character
is corroded and eaten into by daily inconsistency, unfaithfulness and
besetting sin.

F.B. Meyer

How many times do you get to lie before you are a liar?
Michael Josephson

Chapter 2   Integrity

Do not pray for easy lives; pray to be stronger people!
Do not pray for tasks equal to your powers;
pray for power equal to your tasks.
Phillips Brooks
******

How things look on the outside of us
depends on how things are on the inside of us.
Parks Cousins
******

He is no fool who gives what he cannot
keep to gain what he cannot lose.
Jim Elliot
******

Your talent is God's gift to you.
What you do with it is your gift back to God.
Leo Buscaglia

When we hate our enemies, we are giving them power over us: power over our sleep, our appetites, our blood pressure, our health, and our happiness.

Our enemies would dance with joy if only they knew how they were worrying us, lacerating us, and getting even with us! Our hate is not hurting them at all, but our hate is turning our own days and nights into a hellish turmoil.

Dale Carnegie

God has a natural law in force to the effect that we are conformed to that upon which we center our interest and love.
Miles Stanford

Chapter 2   Integrity

Do not lay not up for yourselves treasures on earth, where moth and
rust destroy, and where thieves break in and steal; but lay up for
yourselves treasures in heaven, where neither moth nor rust destroys
and where thieves do not break in and steal. For where your treasure
is, there will your heart be also.
Matthew 6:19-21
******

Do you have call waiting?
When God's call comes in your life - do you put Him on hold?
Not the telephone service - spiritual call waiting?
******

If anyone speaks badly of you, live so none will believe it.
******

Trust in the Lord with all your heart, and lean not on your own
understanding. In all your ways acknowledge Him,
and He shall direct your paths
Proverbs 3:5-6
******

Ideals are like stars; you will not succeed in touching them with your
hands. But like the seafaring man on the desert of waters, you choose
them as your guides, and following them you will reach your destiny.
Carl Schurz
******

They that can give up essential liberty to obtain
a little temporary safety deserve neither liberty nor safety.
Benjamin Franklin
******

It is difficulties that show what men are.
Epicetus

32

Chapter 2   Integrity

A Lasting Legacy

Around the turn of the 19th century, Alfred Nobel's brother died. The local newspaper confused the men and wrote about Alfred's death, instead of his brother's. Alfred was given the rare opportunity to read his own obituary.

It horrified him. Alfred had helped to invent dynamite and in the paper, his obituary emphasized destruction and death, not pleasantries.

Shocked by what he read, Alfred asked friends to define the opposite of destruction. Their response: peace. From that day forward, Alfred concentrated his efforts on working for peace. The Nobel Peace Prize is one his lasting legacies.

To educate a person in mind and not morals
is to educate a menace to society.
Theodore Roosevelt
******

Our background and circumstances may have influenced who we are, but
we are responsible for who we become.
James Rhinehart

A Blessing On A Church Wall: Upwaltham, England

I will not wish thee riches, nor the glow of greatness, but that wherever thou go some weary heart shall gladden at thy smile, or some shadowed life know sunshine for a while. And so thy path shall be a track of light, like angels' footsteps passing through the night.

Chapter 2   Integrity

*Also I heard the voice of the Lord, saying, Whom shall I send, and who
will go for us? Then said I, Here am I; send me.*
Isaiah 6:8
******

The price of greatness is responsibility.
Winston Churchill
******

You cannot do a kindness too soon,
for you never know how soon it will be too late.
Ralph Waldo Emerson
******

The person who does not know how to live while they are making a
living is a poorer person after their wealth
is won than when they started.
Josiah Gilbert Holland
******

*For what profit is it to a man if he gains the whole world,
and lose his own soul? Or what will a man give
in exchange for his soul?*
Matthew 16:26
******

Life gets its meaning, not from self-fulfillment
or success ...... but from a
personal relationship with our Creator.
Charles Colson
******

*If you confess with your mouth Lord Jesus
and believe in your heart that God raised Him
from the dead, you will be saved.*
Romans 10:9a

Chapter 2   Integrity

We and God have business with each other; and in opening ourselves to his influence our deepest destiny is fulfilled. The universe, and those parts of it which our personal being constitutes, takes a turn genuinely for the worse or the better in proportion as each one of us fulfills or evades God's commands.

William Jones

We have committed the Golden Rule to memory;
let us now commit it to life.
Edwin Markham

Every day you may make progress. Every step may be fruitful. Yet there will stretch out before you an ever-lengthening, ever-ascending, ever-improving path. You know you will never get to the end of the journey. But this, so far from discouraging, only adds to the joy and glory of the climb.

Sir Winston Churchill

Crowds cannot make right what God has declared to be wrong.
Neal A. Maxwell
******

As for me, I will call upon God; and the Lord shall save me.
Evening and morning, and at noon,
will I pray, and cry aloud; and He shall hear my voice.
Psalm 55:16-17

Chapter 2   Integrity

There are two ways to live your life. One is as though nothing is a
miracle. The other is as though everything is a miracle.
Albert Einstein
******

Sell not virtue to purchase wealth.
English proverb
******

Therefore, if anyone is in Christ, he is a new creation:
the old have passed away; behold, all things have become new.
2nd Corinthians 5:17

	Take Time
To Think:	It is the source of power
To Work:	It is the price of success
To Play:	It is the secret of perpetual youth
To Read:	It is the fountain of wisdom
To Love and Be Loved:	It is a God-given privilege
To Be Friendly:	It is the road to happiness
To Laugh:	It is the music of the soul.
To Give:	It is too short a day to be selfish
To Pray:	It is the greatest power on earth
To Worship:	It is the soul's great need.

The law of the Lord is perfect, converting the soul; the testimony
of the Lord is sure, making wise the simple. The statutes of
the Lord are right, rejoicing the heart; the command
of the Lord is pure, enlightening the eyes.
Psalm 19:7-8

Chapter 2   Integrity

Let your ears hear what you mouth says.
Jewish Proverb

Mark Twain loved to tell the story of a man who arrived in heaven. Like most people, there were questions he'd always looked forward to asking on that day when he reached his final address.

The man walked up to an angel and said, "I was a keen student of military history. I studied all the great generals of history. Can you tell me who was the greatest of all?

The angel smiles. "That's simple."he said. " It was Fred Jones." And he pointed to a familiar little man nearby.

"Fred Jones," gasped the man. "I knew him! He was only a common factory worker!"

"But, he would have been the greatest general," the angel said, "*if he'd only seen it in himself.*"

You have not lived a perfect day, even though you have
earned your money,   unless you have done something
for someone who cannot repay you.
Ruth Smeltzer
******

It is more shameful to distrust one's friends
than to be deceived by them.
Francois Rochefoucauld
******

Chapter 2   Integrity

It is difficult to make a man miserable while he feels he is worthy of
himself and claims kindred
to the great God who made him.
Abraham Lincoln
******

Most of our faults are more pardonable
than the means we use to conceal them.
Francois Rochefoucauld

A key to the good things in life is running the race in such a way
that you successfully pass the baton. Develop others to serve the Lord
faithfully, spur them on in the faith, and the good you have done will
endure. You will find that your work has not ended, it has only begun.

Charles Stanley

To protect those who are not able to protect themselves
is a duty which every one owes to society.
Edward Macnaghten
******

When you choose the lesser of two evils,
remember that it is still an evil.
Max Lerner
******

Life is the sum of your choices.
Albert Camus

Chapter 2   Integrity

All problems become smaller if you don't dodge them, but confront
them. Touch a thistle timidly, and it pricks you;
grab it boldly, and its spines crumble.
William S. Halsey
******

What worries you, masters you.
Haddon W. Robinson
******

The only way to make a person trustworthy, is to trust them.
Henry L. Stimson

There is a major disaster when a person allows some success to
become a stopping place rather than a way station on to a larger goal. It
often happens that an early success is a greater moral hazard than an early
failure.

Halford E. Luccock

Friendship with oneself is all important, because without it
one cannot be friends with anyone else.
Eleanor Roosevelt

I am not judged by the number of times I fail, but by the number
of times I succeed. And the number of times I succeed is in direct
proportion to the number of times I can fail and keep trying!

Tom Hopkins

Chapter 2   Integrity

The greatest power is often simple patience.
E. Joseph Cossman
******

There is more in us than we know. If we can be
made to see it, perhaps, for the rest of our lives,
we will be unwilling to settle for less.
Kurt Hahn

Success is to be measured not so much by the position that one has
reached in life as by the obstacles that one has overcome while trying to
succeed.

Booker T. Washington

Kind words can be short and easy to speak,
but their echoes are truly endless.
Mother Thesesa
******

Freely you have received, freely give.
Matthew 10:8a
******

The darkest hour in any man's life is when
he sits down to plan how to get money without earning it.
Horace Greeley
******

*No one can serve two masters: for either he will hate the one,
and love the other; or else he will be loyal to the one, and despise the
other. You cannot serve God and mammon.*
Matthew 6:24

Chapter 2   Integrity

The tree of liberty must be refreshed from time to time
with the blood of patriots and tyrants.
Thomas Jefferson

Our Choice
Not what we have, but what we use,
Not what we see, but what we choose:
These are the things that mar or bless
the sum of human happiness.
The thing nearby, not that afar,
Not what we seem, but what we are:
These are the things that make or break,
That give the heart its joy or ache.
Not what seems fair, but what is true,
Not what we dream, but the good we do;
These are the things that shine like gems,
Like stars in fortune's diadems.
Not as we take, but as we give,
Not as we pray, but as we live;
These are the things that make for peace,
Both now and after time shall cease.
Author Unknown

A politician thinks of the next election;
a statesman, of the next generation.
James Freeman Clarke

Chapter 2   Integrity

There are many things in life that will catch your eye,
but only a few will catch your heart ... pursue those.
******

Never mistake knowledge for wisdom.
One helps you make a living; the other helps you make a life.
Sandra Carey
******

America did not invent human rights. In a very real sense,
it is the other way around. Human rights invented America.
Jimmy Carter

The soul is dyed the color of its thoughts. Think only on those
things that are in line with your principles and can bear the full light of
day. The content of your character is your choice. Day by day, what you
choose, what you think, and what you do is who you become. Your
integrity is your destiny ... it is the light that guides your way.

Heraclitus

Jesus said to him, I am the way, the truth, and the life.
No man comes to the Father, except through me.
John 14:6
******

What counts is not necessarily the size of the dog in the fight -
it's the size of the fight in the dog.
Dwight D. Eisenhower
******

People who show you the love of God are "God with skin on."
******

Chapter 2   Integrity

What If .... We put aside the concept that "if only other people would
    behave the way we want them to?"
What If ... We learned early in life that the only reason people change
    their behavior is when they see the need for change?
What If ... Side-stepping our own ego, we learned early that recognizing
    and changing a character weakness is a character strength?
What If ... We attained the serenity that comes from accepting those
    things we cannot change, changing the things we can, and the
    wisdom to know the difference?
What if ... We understood that "to cease to adjust is to cease to
    survive"?

Alan J. Zinser

You cannot believe in honor until you have achieved it.
Better keep yourself clean and bright;
you are the window through which you must see the world.
George Bernard Shaw
******

The wise man must remember that while he is a descendant of the past,
he is parent of the future; and that his thoughts are as children born to
him, which he may not carelessly let die.
Herbert Spencer
******

*For we are His workmanship, created in Christ Jesus
for good works, which God prepared beforehand
that we should walk in them.*
Ephesians 2:10

Chapter 2   Integrity

Some Advice For Living

It's your life, take responsibility for it, don't make excuses.

✓ Life is like a baseball game. Don't go through life bunting. Swing for the fences.

✓ Remember, they are the Ten Commandments, not the Ten Suggestions.

✓ Remember that God is the source of our strength and knowledge. Lean on God.

✓ Remember this story: an old man in a nursing home was asked who he missed most. He said: "The man I could have been." Don't let that happen to you.

✓ Don't do anything twice that you don't want for a habit.

No man is worth is salt who is not ready at all times to risk his body, to risk his well-being, to risk his life, in a great cause.

Theodore Roosevelt

******

Patience is bitter, but its fruit sweet.

Tacitus

******

When a firm, decisive spirit is recognized it is curious
to see how the space clears around a man
and leaves him room and freedom.

John Foster

Chapter 3   Courage

The Dash

I read of a man who stood to speak at the funeral of a friend. He referred to the dates on her tombstone from the beginning .... to the end.

He noted that first came her birth and spoke of the second with tears. But he said what mattered most of all was the dash between those years.

For that dash represented all the time that she spent alive on earth, and now only those who loved her know what that little line is worth.

For it matters not how much we own; the cars, the house, the cash, what matter is how we live and love and how we spend the "dash."

So think about this long and hard: are there things you'd like to change" for you never know how much time is left .... you could be at "dash mid-range."

If we could just slow down and consider what's true and real, and always try to understand the way other people feel.

And be less quick to anger, and show appreciation more - and love the people in our lives like we've never loved before.

If we treat each other with respect, and more often wear a smile, remembering that this special dash might only last a little while.

So, when your eulogy's being read with your life's actions to rehash, would you be pleased with the things they say about how you spent your dash?

Chapter 3

Courage

The word, **Courage**, means having the *mental or moral strength to venture, persevere, and withstand danger, fear, or difficulty; mental or moral strength to resist opposition, danger, or hardship.* The word, courage, derives from the Latin word [*cor*] meaning heart.

Synonyms for courage include: endurance, mettle, resolve, determination, spirit, bravery, gumption, spunk, and tenacity.

Courage does not mean the absence of fear. Courage means overcoming fear through confidence and trust in God's sovereignty, omnipresence, and omnipotence. His strength is sufficient in every situation we face.

As we read and study God's Word , memorizing key verses, and meditating on their meaning, we will find that our courage comes by relying on God's presence, power and guidance

This book of the Law shall not depart from your mouth, but you shall meditate in it day and night, that you may observe to do according to all that is written in it. For then you will make your way prosperous, and then you will have good success. Have I not commanded you? Be strong of good courage; do not be afraid, nor be dismayed, for the Lord Your God is with you wherever you go.
Joshua 1:8-9

Chapter 3   Courage

Even though I walk through the valley of the shadow of death,
I will fear no evil for you are with me; your rod and your staff,
they comfort me. You prepare a table before me
in the presence of my enemies.
Psalm 23:4-5
***
***

God is our refuge and strength,
an ever-present help in times of trouble.
Psalm 46:1
******

When we are dis-couraged, we are out of courage, and we need
to come back to God, get on our knees and get a fresh supply.
******

Courage is being scared to death —— and saddling up anyway.
John Wayne

The One In The Glass

If you get what you want in your struggle for self,
And the world makes you a champion for a day,
Just go to the mirror and look at yourself,
And see what that person has to say.
For it isn't your father, or mother, or brother,
Who upon you their judgment will pass.
The person whose verdict counts most in your life
Is the one staring back from the glass......
He or she is the one to please——never mind all the rest!
For he or she is with you right up to the end.
And you've passed your most difficult test,
If the person in the glass is your friend.
You may fool the world down the pathway of years,
And get pats on the back, as you pass,
But your final reward will be headaches or tears,
If you've cheated the one in the glass.

Chapter 3   Courage

Fear not, for I am with you, be not dismayed, for I am your God;
I will strengthen you, yes, I will help you,
I will uphold you with my righteous right hand.
Isaiah 41:10
******

It's never too late to become what you might have been.
George Eliot
******

I am only one. But still, I am one.
I cannot do everything. But I can do something.
And, because I cannot do everything, I will not refuse to do what I can.
Edwin Hale

> I honor any man who in the conscious discharge of his duty dares to stand alone; the world, with ignorant, intolerant judgment, may condemn; the countenance of relatives may be averted, and the hearts of friends grow cold; but the sense of duty done shall be sweeter than the applause of the world, the countenances of relatives, or the hearts of friends.
>
> Charles Sumner

Blessed is the man who endures temptation,
for when he has been approved, he will receive
the crown of life which the Lord has promised to those who love Him.
James 1:12
******

One man with courage makes a majority.
Andrew Jackson
******

It is better to die on one's feet than to live on one's knees.
Albert Camus

Chapter 3   Courage

Cowards die many times before their deaths;
the valiant never taste of death but once.
William Shakespeare
******
Truth and love are two of the most powerful things in the world;
and when they both go together they cannot easily be withstood.
Ralph Cudworth

Keep Swimming

Two frogs fell into a deep cream bowl. One was an optimistic soul. But the other took the gloomy view. "We'll drown," he lamented without much ado, and with a last despairing cry, he flung up his legs and said "Goodbye."

Quote the other frog with a steadfast grin, "I can't get out but I won't give in, I'll just swim around till my strength is spent, then I'll die the more content." Bravely he swam to work his scheme, and his struggles began to churn the cream.

The more he swam, his legs a flutter, the more the cream turned into butter. On top of the butter at last he stopped, and out of the bowl he gaily hopped.

What is the moral? It's easily found... If you can't hop out, keep swimming around!

Author Unknown

If God is for us, who can be against us?

Romans 8:31a

Chapter 3   Courage

The reasonable man adapts himself to the world;

the unreasonable one persists in trying to adapt the world

to himself. Therefore all progress depends on the unreasonable man.

George Bernard Shaw

******

We can easily forgive a child who is afraid of the dark;

the real tragedy of life is when men are afraid of the light.

Plato

The Winner

It is not the critic who counts, not the man who points out how the strong man stumbled or where the doer of deeds could have done better.

The credit belongs to the man who is actually in the arena; whose face is marred by dust and sweat and blood; who strives valiantly; who errs and comes short again and again; who knows the great enthusiasms, the great devotions, and spends himself in a worthy cause; who, at best, knows in the end the triumph of high achievement; and who, at the worst, if he fails, at least fails while daring greatly, so that his place shall never be with those cold and timid souls who know neither victory nor defeat.

Theodore Roosevelt

The Lord is my light and my salvation. Who is there to fear?

The Lord is my life's fortress. Who is there to be afraid of?

Psalm 27:1

Chapter 3   Courage

Our greatest glory is not in never failing,

but in rising up every time we fail.

Ralph Waldo Emerson

Let Your Light Shine

There is a story of a young man who felt overcome by a sense of despair when he thought of all the injustice, pain and cruelty in the world. When he went to his place of worship he prayed: "Oh Lord, I don't understand. How can you allow all this injustice, pain and cruelty and do nothing?"

Getting no reply, he asks again in an audible voice, "How can you do nothing." Then he heard a small voice from behind say, "He didn't do nothing, he made you."

What a powerful and profound insight it is when you realize that you are God's instrument for a better world.

Courage is fear that has said its prayers.

******

The Lord bless you and keep you;

The Lord make his face shine upon you, and be gracious to you;

the Lord lift up his countenance upon you, and give you peace.

Numbers 6:24-26

Chapter 3   Courage

He jests at scars that never felt a wound.

Shakespeare

******

It is not enough for a man to know how to ride,

he must also know how to fall.

Native American Proverb

You cannot be, I know, nor do I wish to see you, an inactive
spectator ... We have too many high sounding words and too few actions
that correspond with them.

Abigail Adams

[writing to her husband, John Adams, prior to the American Revolution]

We know that all things work together for the good of those who love
God - those whom He has called according to His plan.

Romans 8:28

******

Keep your fears to yourself, but share your courage with others.

Robert Louis Stevenson

******

He who walks with wise men will be wise,

but the companions of fools will be destroyed.

Proverbs 13:20

Chapter 3   Courage

It is better to suffer wrong than to do it, and
happier to be sometimes cheated than not to trust.

Samuel Johnson

******

Cast your burden on the Lord, and He shall sustain you:
He shall never permit the righteous to be moved.

Psalm 55:22

I Asked......

I asked God for strength, that I might achieve;

I was made weak, that I might learn humbly to obey.

I asked for health, that I might do great things;

I was given infirmity, that I might do better things.

I asked for riches, that I might be happy;

I was given poverty, that I might be wise.

I asked for power, that I might have the praise of men;

I was given weakness, that I might feel the need of God.

I asked for all things, that I might enjoy life;

I was given life, that I might enjoy all things.

I got nothing that I asked for - but everything I had hoped for.

Almost despite myself, my unspoken prayers were answered.

I am, among all men, most richly blessed.

Anonymous

Chapter 3   Courage

People of principle will not do on the job
what they will not do at home.

The Cross

The young man was at the end of his rope. Seeing no way out, he dropped to his knees in prayer. "Lord, I can't go on," he said. "I have too heavy a cross to bear."

The Lord replied, "My son, if you can't bear its weight, just place your cross inside this room. Then, open that other door and pick out any cross you wish."

The man was filled with relief. "Thank you, Lord," he sighed, and he did as he was told.

Upon entering the other door, he saw many crosses; some so large the tops were not visible. Then, he spotted a tiny cross leaning against a far wall. "I'd like that one, Lord," he whispered.

The Lord replied, "My son, that is the cross you just brought in."

Author Unknown

I'd rather be a could-be, if I cannot be an are,

because a could-be is a maybe, who is reaching for a star.

I'd rather be a has-been, than a might-have-been by far,

for a might-have-been has never been,

but a has-been was once an are.

Milton Berle

Chapter 3   Courage

...This is what the Lord says to you. 'Do not be afraid or discouraged...
for the battle is not yours, but God's'.

2 Chronicles 20:15

What Became of the Twelve Disciples?	
Andrew	Died on a cross at Patros, in Acchia
Bartholomew	Was flogged alive in Albanapolis, Armenia
Simon	Died on a cross in Persia
Judas Iscariot	After betraying Jesus, he hanged himself
Peter	Was crucified, head downward, during the persecution by Nero
Thomas	Was run through with a lance in Coromandel, in the East Indies
Philip	Was hanged against a pillar at Neropolis, a city of Phyrgia in Asia Minor
Matthew	Was slain by the sword in Ethiopia
Thaddeus	Was shot to death with arrows
James	Younger brother of the Savior, was thrown from the pinnacle of the Temple, and then beaten to death with a club
James	The elder son of Zebedee, was beheaded in Jerusalem
John	Died of old age in Ephesus

Chapter 3   Courage

The Eagle

Did you know that an eagle knows when a storm is approaching long before it breaks?

The eagle will fly to some high spot and wait for the winds to come. When the storm hits, it sets its wings so that the wind will pick it up and lift it above the storm. While the storm rages below, the eagle is soaring above it.

The eagle does not escape the storm. It simply uses the storm to lift it higher. It rises on the winds that bring the storm. When the storms of life come upon us -and all of us will experience them - we can rise above them by setting our minds and our belief toward God.

The storms do not have to overcome us. We can allow God's power to lift us above them. God enables us to ride the winds of the storm that bring sickness, tragedy, failure and disappointment in our lives. We can soar above the storm.

Remember, it is not the burdens of life that weigh us down, it is how we handle them. The Bible says, *"Those who hope in the Lord will renew their strength. They will soar on wings like eagles."* Isaiah 40:31.

We are not at our best when we are perched at the summit;

we are at our best climbing - even when the way is steep.

******

He who accepts evil without protesting

against it is really cooperating with it!

George Matheson, Scottish author and preacher, who was blind, expressed this prayer:

"I have thanked Thee a thousand times for my roses, but never once for my 'thorn' ... Teach me the glory of my cross; teach me the value of my 'thorn.' Show me that I have climbed to Thee by the path of pain. Show me that my tears have made my rainbow."

Let us endeavor so to live that when we come to die

even the undertaker will be sorry.

Mark Twain

******

To him who is in fear, everything rustles.

Sophocles

******

In taking revenge, a man is equal to his enemy;

in passing over it, he is superior.

******

It is better to trust in the LORD than to put confidence in man.

Psalms 118:8

Chapter 3   Courage

An optimist is ....

A person who is happy to be alive even at sad moments.
A person who knows that it isn't the victory but the fight that makes
a man.
A person who assumes his responsibilities and mistakes before
being asked to do so.
A person who knows that you have to plant first and then harvest.
A person who can keep his head up even after failure.
A person who knows that the glory is in the actions and not in the
advantages the actions can bring.
A person who worries about not deceiving others.
A person who knows that the peace we seek for can only be found
inside our hearts.
A person who knows that it's not worth it to bury our deceptions on
futility.
A person who knows that our defects come mainly from our own   weaknesses.
A person who knows how to be gentle and polite.
A person who knows how to respect himself without disrespecting
others.
A person who knows that the bad moments are not here to stay and
therefore keeps the faith.
A person who can forget the cruelty of friends and relatives.
A person who knows how to wait without getting desperate.
A person who speaks to God in the immensity of His love.
A person who can see the brightness in a child's eye even in the darkness.
                    Unknown Author

Chapter 3   Courage

In reading the lives of great men, I found that

the first victory they won was over themselves ...

self-discipline with all of them came first.

Harry S. Truman

******

Never confuse the will of the majority with the will of God.

Charles Colson

How Well Do You Know The Shepherd?

There is a story of an English actor who was honored at a banquet. During the course of the evening, he was asked to give a reading, and he chose Psalm 23, about the Good Shepherd.

He read it with great eloquence and clear enunciation, and received a great deal of applause.

Later in the evening, an older clergyman was asked to speak. He, too, recited Psalm 23. His voice rang with assurance and was vibrant with love. When he concluded, there was no applause, but there was hardly a dry eye.

The actor rose to grasp the minister's hand and said, "Sir, I know the Psalm, but you know the Shepherd."

I would ask you, "How well do you know the Shepherd?   At what stage are you in your discipleship? Are you being nurtured so that you can produce fruit?

59

Chapter 3   Courage

The optimist sees opportunity in every danger;

the pessimist sees danger in every opportunity.

Winston Churchill

******

..we also glory in tribulations, knowing that tribulation produces
perseverance; and perseverance, character; and character, hope.

Romans 5:3a

******

Do not be overcome by evil, but overcome evil with good

Romans 12:21

******

He who has lost confidence can lose nothing more.

Boiste

******

Words which do not give the light of Christ increase the darkness.

Mother Teresa

******

Trouble is the structural steel

that goes into building character.

Chapter 3   Courage

Talking or Doing?

All of us must get out of the rut of just talking about missions and witnessing, but doing nothing about it. Pastor Horace Bushnell [1802-1876] wrote:

The following are excused from giving or going:

1.   Those who believe the world is lost and does not need a Savior;

2.   Those who wish the missionaries had never come to our ancestors, and that we ourselves were still heathens;

3.   Those who believe that it is 'every man for himself' in this world, and who, with Cain, ask, "Am I my brother's keeper?'

4.   Those who believe they are not accountable to God for the money entrusted to them;

   a.   Those who are prepared to accept the final sentence, *"Inasmuch as you did not do it to one of the least of these, you did not do it to Me'* Matthew 25:4

He who does not have the courage to speak up

for his rights cannot earn the respect of others.
Renéé G. Torres

Chapter 3   Courage

If you will trust in God, it must not be when your enemies are few and your coffers are full. It is when your adversaries have mounted and stomach is growling that you prove your belief in God.

Charles Stanley

******

Be anxious for nothing, but in everything by prayer and supplication with thanksgiving let your requests be made known to God.

Philipians 4:6

The Winner is always a part of the answer; The Loser is always a part of the problem.

The Winner always has a program; The Loser always has an excuse.

The Winner says, "Let me do it for you;" The Loser says, "That's not my job."

The Winner sees an answer for every problem; The Loser sees a problem in every answer.

The Winner says, "It may be difficult but it's possible;" The Loser says, "It may be possible but it's too difficult"

Jesus stood and cried out, saying, If any man thirst,

let him come unto me, and drink.

John 7:37b

Chapter 3   Courage

Do what you can with what you have where you are.

Theodore Roosevelt

There is a story of a man who once stood before God, his heart breaking from the pain and injustice in the world.

"Dear God," he cried out, "look at all the suffering, the anguish and distress in the world. Why don't you send help?"

God responded, "I did send help. I sent you."

David J. Wolfe

You can't escape the responsibility of tomorrow by evading it today.

Abraham Lincoln

******

I am the light of the world. He who follows Me

shall not walk in darkness, but have the light of life.

John 8:12

******

He who loses wealth loses much;

He who loses a friend loses more;

But he that loses his courage loses all.

Miquel de Cervantes

Chapter 3   Courage

It is easy to take liberty for granted
if you have never had it taken away from you.
Dick Cheney
******

Let us have the faith that right makes might;
and in that faith let us, to the end,
dare to do our duty as we understand it.
Abraham Lincoln
******

For God has not given us a spirit of fear;
but of power, and of love, and of a sound mind.
2nd Timothy 1:7
******

Have not I commanded you? Be strong and of a good courage;
do not be afraid, nor be dismayed;
for the Lord your God is with you wherever you go.
Joshua 1:9
******

Courage is doing what you're afraid to do.
There can be no courage unless you're scared.
Eddie Rickenbacker

Chapter 3   Courage

Freedom Is Never Free

What happened to the 56 men who signed the Declaration of Independence? These were not wild-eyed, rabble-rousing ruffians. They had security, but they valued liberty more. Standing tall, straight, and unwavering, they pledged: "For the support of this declaration, with firm reliance on the protection of the divine providence, we mutually pledge to each other, our lives, our fortunes, and our sacred honor."

Five signers were captured by the British as traitors, and tortured before they died. Twelve had their homes ransacked and burned. Two lost their sons serving in the Revolutionary Army; another had two sons captured. Nine of the 56 fought and died from wounds or hardships of the Revolutionary War.

What kind of men were they? Twenty-four were lawyers and jurists. Eleven were merchants, nine were farmers and large plantation owners; men of means, well educated. They signed the Declaration of Independence knowing full well that the penalty would be death if they were captured.

Carter Brixton of Virginia, a wealthy planter and trader, saw his ships swept from the seas by the British Navy. He sold his home and properties to pay his debts, and died in rags.

Thomas McKeam was so hounded by the British that he was forced to move his family almost constantly. He served in the Congress without pay, and his family was kept in hiding. His possessions were taken from him, and poverty was his reward. ·

Vandals or soldiers looted the properties of Dillery, Hall, Clymer, Walton, Gwinnett, Heyward, Ruttledge, and Middleton. Thomas Nelson Jr, noting that the British General Cornwallis had his home for headquarters, quietly urged General George Washington to open fire. The home was destroyed, and Nelson died bankrupt.

Francis Lewis had his home and properties destroyed. The enemy jailed his wife, and she died within a few months. John Hart was driven from his wife's bedside as she was dying. For more than a year he lived in forests and caves, returning home to find his wife dead and his children vanished. A few weeks later he died from exhaustion and a broken heart. Norris and Livingston suffered similar fates.

Chapter 3   Courage

Yea, though I walk through the valley of the shadow of death,
I will fear no evil, for You are with me;
Your rod and Your staff they comfort me.
You prepare a table before me in the presence of my enemies.
Psalm 23:4-5

Chapter 4

Attitude

The word, **Attitude** is defined as a state of mind or feeling with regard to some matter. Some common synonyms for attitude include: outlook, perspective, insight, judgment, viewpoint, mood, and opinion.

The word, attitude, comes from the Italian *attitudine,* literally, aptitude, from Late Latin *aptitudin - aptitude -* fitness.

We all have an attitude. Whether or not our attitude is positive or negative, however, influences how we meet life's challenges. With a positive attitude - one that seeks the same attitude Christ would have - we have a standard of behavior that keeps us close to God.

God has a purpose for each of our lives, and, as we submit our talents, and lives to Him, His personality will begin to appear in our daily lives. Having an attitude of gratitude for our salvation, paid for by Jesus Christ's blood, enables us to seek ways each day to glorify God.

In the New Testament, there are only two commandments, compared to the Ten Commandments, and the Mosaic Law.

In Mark 12, vv 30-31, Jesus tells the Pharisee which commandment was most important

Mark 12:30 *And you shall love the Lord your God with all your heart and with all your soul and with all your mind and with all your strength.*

Mark 12:31 *And the second is this: You shall love your neighbor as yourself. There is no other commandment greater than these.*

Chapter 4   Attitude

I can do all things through Christ who strengthens me.

Philippians 4:13

******

This is the day the Lord has made,

we will rejoice and be glad in it.

Psalm 118:24

In the "Peanuts" comic strip, Peppermint Patty once asked Charlie Brown if he knew any good rules for living. This was his list:

- Keep the ball low
- Don't leave your crayons in the sun
- Use dental floss every day
- Don't let the ants get in the sugar
- Always get your first serve in

If you think you can, or you think you can't,

you're probably right.

Henry Ford

******

To respect yourself is the beginning of one of life's greatest attitudes.

******

Commit your works to the Lord, and your thoughts will be established.

Proverbs 16:3

Chapter 4   Attitude

Shake It Off and Step Up

A parable is told of a farmer who owned an old mule. The mule fell into the farmer's well. The farmer heard the mule 'braying' - or - whatever mules do when they fall into wells. After carefully assessing the situation, the farmer sympathized with the mule, but decided that neither the mule nor the well was worth the trouble of saving. Instead, he called his neighbors together and told them what had happened and enlisted them to help haul dirt to bury the old mule in the well and put him out of his misery.

Initially, the old mule was hysterical! But as the farmer and his neighbors continued shoveling and the dirt hit his back, a thought struck him. It suddenly dawned on him that every time a shovel load of dirt landed on his back: **he should shake it off and step up!** This he did, blow after blow.

"Shake it off and step up... shake it off and step up... shake it off and step up!" he repeated to encourage himself. No matter how painful the blows, or distressing the situation seemed the old mule fought "panic" and just kept right on **shaking it off and stepping up!**

You're right! It wasn't long before the old mule, battered and exhausted, stepped triumphantly over the wall of that well! What seemed like it would bury him, actually blessed him. All because of the manner in which he handled his adversity.

Unknown

Attitude is everything: Most people looked at Goliath
and said, "He's too big to fight." David looked at Goliath
and said, "He's too big to miss."

Chapter 4   Attitude

Attitude is the polish that determines
how much our aptitude shines.
Robert F. Litro

******

I don't know the key to success,
but the key to failure is trying to please everybody.
Bill Cosby

******

Write the bad things that are done to you in sand, but write the good
things that happen to you on a piece of marble.
Arabic Parable

******

If someone were to pay you ten cents for every kind word that
you have spoken about people, and collect from you five cents
for every unkind word, would you be rich or poor?

*****

The best and most beautiful things in the world cannot
be seen or even touched.   They must be felt with the heart.
Helen Keller

******

It is a funny thing about life: if you refuse
to accept anything but the best, you very often get it.
W. Somerset Maugham

Chapter 4   Attitude

Twenty years from now you will be more disappointed
by the things you didn't do than by the ones you did.
So throw off the bowlines, sail away from the safe harbor.
Catch the trade winds in your sails. Explore. Dream.
Mark Twain
******

Keep your heart with all diligence, for out of it spring the issues of life.
Proverbs 4:23

To laugh often and much; to win the

respect of intelligent people

and the affection of children;

to earn the appreciation of honest critics

and endure the betrayal of false friends;

to appreciate beauty, to find the best in others;

to leave the world a little better;

whether by a healthy child, a garden patch or a redeemed social

condition; to know even one life has breathed easier

because you have lived.

This is the meaning of success.

Ralph Waldo Emerson

Chapter 4   Attitude

No one can make you feel inferior without your permission.

Eleanor Roosevelt

******

When I was a boy of fourteen, my father was so ignorant I could hardly stand to have the old man around. But when I got to be twenty-one, I was astonished at how much the old man had learned in seven years.

Mark Twain

******

I praise loudly, I blame softly.

Catherine the Great

In the Sahara desert, two travelers stopped their Land Rover beside a man who was running along wearing only swimming trunks. "I'm on the way to have a swim," the man told them. "But the sea is more that 500 miles from here!" exclaimed one of the travelers.

"Five hundred miles?" the would-be bather shouted. "What a terrific beach!"

Happiness is not a state to arrive at, but a manner of traveling.
Margaret Lee Runbeck
******
Humble people don't think less of themselves -
they just think about themselves less.

Chapter 4   Attitude

If you are not big enough to lose, you are not big enough to win.
Walter Reuther
******

Before destruction the heart of a man
is haughty, and before honor is humility.
Proverbs 18:12
******

Once you have accepted yourself, it's so much easier
to accept other people and their points of view.
******

For if you forgive men their trespasses,
your heavenly Father will also forgive you.
If you do not forgive men their trespasses,
neither will your Father forgive your trespasses.
Matthew 6:14-15
******

The primary purpose of education is not to teach you
to earn your bread, but to make every mouthful sweeter.
******

Have you had a kindness shown? Pass it on!
Let it travel down the years. Let it wipe another's tears.
Till in Heaven the deed appears - Pass it on.
******

The glory of life is to love, not be loved,
to give, not to get; to serve, not to be served.
******

God gave us two ends. One to sit on and one to think with.
Success depends on which one you use; heads you win--tails, you lose.
Anonymous

Chapter 4   Attitude

People who treat other people as less than human
must not be surprised when the bread they have cast
on the waters comes floating back to them, poisoned.
James Baldwin
******

In the tough times, remember Karl Wallenda. Karl was the patriarch of the Wallenda family, internationally known for their high-wire walking exploits. Karl fell 120 feet to his death while trying to walk a tight-wire between two office buildings in Puerto Rico.

Later, his wife said that before the stunt, for the first time in his life, Karl had seemed concerned about falling. When it came time to perform, he fell because he was so focused on not falling, rather than on getting to the other side.

Moral: when you concentrate on not losing, rather than on winning, you'll find yourself dead on the ground.

Whoever shuts his ears to the cry of the poor,
will also cry out and not be heard.
Proverbs 21:13
******

All who would win joy must share it; happiness was born a twin.
******

The Lord sees not only how much we give, but also how much we keep.
*****

The spirit, the will to win, and the will to excel are things that endure.
These qualities are so much more important than the events that occur.
Vince Lombardi

We Get What We Expect

A family was traveling through a town some distance from here recently, and stopped at a general store. The young father spoke to an old man sitting in front of the store.

"Excuse me sir," he asked, "what kind of people settled out here." "What kind of people are they where you came from," asked the old man.

The young father replied, "They are mean, full of mischief, and small-minded."

"Sorry to say, young feller, but that's the kind of folks you'll find out here," replied the old man.

Later in the week, another family pulled into the same town, and stopped at the same general store. The old man was there sitting in front of the store.

"Excuse me sir," asked the young father, "what kind of people settled out here?"

The old man replied again, "What kind of people are they where you came from?"

This young father replied, "The people we left behind are kind, decent people who are very generous."

"Well, my friend, you've come to the right place, because those are the kind of people you're going to find here," replied the old man with a kindly smile.

Let the words of my mouth and the meditation of my heart
be acceptable in Your sight, O, Lord, my strength and my Redeemer.
Psalm 19:14
******

Opportunity is missed by most people
because it is dressed in overalls and looks like work.
Thomas Edison

Chapter 4   Attitude

Ten Commandments For Losers   by John R. Graham

1.   Always have an excuse
   ✓ Never be caught speechless when it comes to making excuses
      for yourself

2.   Be sure to blend into the pack
   ✓ It is important to remain invisible, never call attention to
      yourself

3.   Keep your eye on the competition
   ✓ Never think about your clients or customers

4.   Avoid taking risks at all costs
   ✓ Risk takers lead the pack by always wanting to test
      themselves they want to do better

5.   Never let yourself become enthusiastic
   ✓ If you do, you'll want to become more involved in your work
      and place your company, co-workers and customers
      ahead of yourself

6.   Always put yourself first
   ✓ Before doing anything, ask "What's in it for me?"

7.   If something goes wrong, blame someone
   ✓ Taking responsibilities causes difficulties, so make sure you
      always have someone to blame when a problem arises

8.   Spend a lot of time second-guessing the boss.
   ✓ This is a top priority, never show any initiative so you are
      guaranteed a spot at the bottom of the ladder

9.   Never learn anything new
   ✓ Knowledge is dangerous! It means you will become a problem
      solver

10.   If all else fails, say "I don't know"
   ✓ The less you know, the better off you are - you'll quickly
      become useless

Chapter 4   Attitude

The tragedy of life is not that it ends so soon,
but that we wait so long to begin it.
Richard L. Evans
******

Most people are about as happy as they
make up their minds to be.
Abraham Lincoln
*****

Do not let unwholesome talk come out of your mouths,
but only what is helpful for building others up according to their needs...
Ephesians 4:29
******

In the presence of trouble, some people
grow wings; others buy crutches.

Thou that has given so much to me.

Give one thing more – a grateful heart;

Not thankful when it pleaseth me.

As if Thy blessings had spare days;

But such a heart, whose pulse may be Thy praise.

George Herbert

My business is not to remake myself, but to make the
absolute best of what God made.
Robert Browning
******

It doesn't matter when you start, as long as you start now.
Edward Deming

Chapter 4   Attitude

If you find yourself growing angry at someone, pray for him - anger cannot live in an atmosphere of prayer.
W.T. McElroy
******

Fear knocked at the door. Faith opened it to find no one there.
******

I'd rather one should walk with me, than merely show the way.
Edgar A. Guest
******

God made you as you are in order to use you as He planned.
S.C. McAulay

Seize The Day!

Imagine there is a bank which credits your account each morning with $86,400. It carries over no balance from day to day, allows you to keep no cash balance, and every evening cancels whatever part of the amount you had failed to use during the day.

What would you do? Draw out every cent, of course!

Well, everyone has such a bank. Its name is TIME. Every morning, it credits you with 86,400 seconds. Every night it writes off, as a lost, whatever of this amount you have failed to invest to good purpose. It carries over no balance. It allows no overdraft. Each day it opens a new account for you. Each night it burns the records of the day.

If you fail to use the day's deposits, the loss is yours. There is no going back. There is no drawing against the "tomorrow". You must live in the present on today's deposits.

Invest it so as to get from it the utmost in health, happiness sand success! The clock is running. Make the most of today.

Seize the day!

Chapter 4   Attitude

Great works are not performed by strength, but by perseverance.
Samuel Johnson
******

... Let us run with endurance the race that is set before us,
looking unto Jesus, the author and finisher of our faith...
Hebrews 12:1b-2
******

So teach us to number our days, that we may gain a heart of wisdom.
Psalm 90:12
******

The man who has nothing to boast of but his illustrious ancestors
is like a potato - the only good belonging to him is underground.
Sir Thomas Overbury
******

Many people make a grave mistake by burying their gifts.
******

Difficulties are things that show what men are.
Epicetus
******

A man should never be ashamed to say he has been wrong,
which is but saying in others words that
he is wiser today than he was yesterday.
Alexander Pope
******

For God so loved the world that He gave His only
begotten Son, that whoever believes in Him
should not perish but have everlasting life.
John 3:16

We are all manufacturers: some people are
making good; some people are making trouble;
and some people are making excuses.
******

There are no shortcuts to anywhere worth going.
Beverly Sills
******

Don't be sad about the things you want and don't get.
Think about how many things you don't want that you don't get!

The Power of Choice

The power of choice is real.

We can . . .

Choose to love--rather than hate.
Choose to smile--rather than frown.
Choose to build--rather than destroy.
Choose to persevere--rather than quit.
Choose to praise--rather than gossip.
Choose to heal--rather than wound.
Choose to give--rather than grasp.
Choose to act--rather than delay.
Choose to pray--rather than despair.
Choose to forgive--rather than curse.

Each day brings a new opportunity to choose. What kind of choices will you make today?

Fr. Norbert Weber

Chapter 4   Attitude

Every exit is an entry somewhere else.
Tom Stoppard
******

What we see depends mainly on what we look for.
John Lubbock
******

The fear of the Lord is the beginning of knowledge,
but fools despise wisdom and instruction.
Proverbs 1:7
******

Notice the difference between what happens when a man
says to himself, I have failed three times,
and what happens when he says, I am a failure.
S.I. Hayakawa

Refusing To Accept Failure

Sir Edmund Hillary was the first man to climb Mount Everest. On May 29, 1953 he scaled the highest mountain then known to man-29,000 feet straight up. He was knighted for his efforts. He even made American Express card commercials because of it! However, until we read his book, High Adventure, we don't understand that Hillary had to grow into this success.

You see, in 1952, he attempted to climb Mount Everest, but failed. A few weeks later a group in England asked him to address its members. Hillary walked on stage to a thunderous applause. The audience was recognizing an attempt at greatness, but Edmund Hillary saw himself as a failure. He moved away from the microphone and walked to the edge of the platform.

He made a fist and pointed at a picture of the mountain. He said in a loud voice, "Mount Everest, you beat me the first time, but I'll beat you the next time because you've grown all you are going to grow... but I'm still growing!"

Brian Cavanaugh

Chapter 4   Attitude

There are two kinds of failures: those who thought
and never did, and those who did and never thought.
Lawrence J. Peters
******

Life is not so short but that there is always room for courtesy.
Ralph Waldo Emerson
******

If we have no peace, it is because we
have forgotten that we belong to each other.
Mother Teresa
******

Keep away from people who try to belittle your ambitions.
Small people always do that, but the really great
make you feel that you, too, can become great.
Mark Twain

Buttoning Our Shirt: Starting Right

Have you ever buttoned your shirt, and placed the first button in the wrong button hole. We quickly learn that we can not start wrong and come out right.

How we begin something is of utmost importance. Each of us stands today at the beginning of our future....

We cannot change what has happened, but we can change what will happen.

Growing old is mandatory, growing up is optional.
******
The best place to find a helping hand
is at the end of your own arm.
Swedish proverb

Chapter 4   Attitude

We do not stop playing because we are old;

we are old because we stop playing.

******

It is the greatest of all mistakes to do nothing

because you can only do a little. Do what you can.

Sydney Smith

******

The smallest deed is better than the greatest intention.

******

Gratitude is the memory of the heart.

******

I am dissatisfied with my performance,

I am not dissatisfied with myself.

******

A problem is a chance for you to do your best.

Duke Ellington

*****

There can be no happiness if the things we believe in

are different from the things we do.

******

Ignorance is a voluntary misfortune.

Italian Proverb

Chapter 4   Attitude

The Indispensable Man

Sometimes when you're feeling important, sometimes when your ego is in bloom....Sometimes when you begin to think you're most qualified in the room.

Sometimes when you think your going would leave an unfillable hole. Just follow these simple instructions and see how they humble your soul. Take a bucket and fill it with water. Stick your hand in it up to the wrist.

Pull it out, and the hole which remains is the measure of how you'll be missed. You can splash all you want as you enter, you can stir up the water galore. But stop and you'll see in a moment, it looks quite as calm as before.

Now the moral of this quaint example is: "Do the best that you can!" Be proud of yourself, but remember - there's no indispensable man!

Anonymous

We can do no great things, only small things with great love.

Mother Teresa

******

The person who is waiting for something to turn up

might start with their shirt sleeves.

Garth Henrichs

Chapter 5
Habit

The word, **Habit**, refers to a constant, often unconscious inclination, or tendency, to perform some act, acquired through frequent repetition. It is an established trend of the mind or character that has become nearly or completely involuntary.

Some of the more common synonyms for habit include: pattern, routine, custom, tendency, conduct, dependence, craving, and fixation. The word, habit, comes from the Latin: *habitus* - condition, character, from *habere:* to have, or to hold.

Our habits can either help us to victory, or send us to defeat. What we are, and what we become, is, after all, the sum of our habits. The habit sequence go like this: our thoughts give rise to our actions, our actions become our habits, the sum of our habits becomes our character, and our character become our destiny.

By understanding and submitting to God's Word, we can meet and fend off the appearance of Satan's menace and deceit. God's Word provides us with the perseverance to pursue holiness by recalling what God has asked us to do, and claiming His Grace to do it.

Your word is a lamp for my feet, and a light for my path.

Psalm 119:10

Chapter 5   Habit

And whatever you do, in word or deed,
do all in the name of the Lord Jesus,
giving thanks to God the Father through Him..
Colossians 3:17

******

Whoever can be trusted with very little can also be trusted
with much, and whoever is dishonest with very little
will also be dishonest with much.
Luke 16:10

******

Leisure is a beautiful garment,
but it will not do for constant wear.

******

We too often love things and use people, when we should
be using things and loving people.

******

We are what we repeatedly do.
Excellence, then, is not an act, but a habit.
Aristotle

Chapter 5   Habit

Five Short Chapters On Change

Chapter 1. I walk down a street and there's a deep hole in the sidewalk. I fall in. It takes forever to get out. It's my fault.

Chapter 2. I walk down the same street. I fall in the hole again. It still takes a long time to get out. It's not my fault.

Chapter 3. I walk down the same street. I fall in the hole again. It's becoming a habit. It is my fault. I get out immediately.

Chapter 4. I walk down the same street and see the deep hole in the sidewalk. I walk around it.

Chapter 5. I walk down a different street.

Don't make the mistake of letting yesterday

use up too much of today.

******

Whoever wants to be the most important person

must take the last place and be a servant to everyone else.

Mark 9:35b

The door to happiness is outward.

Chapter 5   Habit

The law of the Lord is perfect, reviving the soul.
The statutes of the Lord are trustworthy, making wise the simple.

Psalm 19:7

******

Habit is a cable; we weave a thread of it every day,

and at last we can not break it.

Horace Mann

Watch your thoughts; they become words.

Watch your words; they become actions.

Watch your actions; they become habits.

Watch your habits; they become character.

Watch your character; it becomes your destiny.

Frank Outlaw

The only exercise some people get is jumping at conclusions,

running down their friends, sidestepping responsibility,

and pushing their luck.

******

We may give without loving, but we cannot love without giving.

Chapter 5   Habit

If any of you lack wisdom, he should ask God, who gives
generously to all without finding fault, and it will be given him.

James 1:5

Who Am I?

You may know me. I'm your constant companion. I'm your greatest helper, I'm your heaviest burden. I will push you onward or drag you down to failure. I am at your command.

Half the tasks you do might as well be turned over to me. I'm able to do them quickly and I'm able to do them the same every time if that's what you want.

I'm easily managed, all you've got to do is be firm with me. Show me exactly how you want it done; after a few lessons I'll do it automatically.

I am the servant of all great men and women; of course, servant of the failures as well. I've made all the great individuals who have ever been great. And, I've made all the failures, too.

I work with all the precision of a marvelous computer with the intelligence of a human being. You may run me for profit or you may run me to ruin, it makes no difference to me. Take me. Be easy with me and I will destroy you.

Be firm with me and I'll put the world at your feet. Who am I?

I'm Habit!

Chapter 5   Habit

The greatest calamity is not to have failed, but to have failed to try.

******

Happiness is like a kiss: you must share it to have it.

******

Too many folks go through life running from
something that isn't after them.

******

Blessed is the person who trusts the Lord,
The Lord will be his confidence.

Jeremiah 17:7

******

There is a vast difference between putting
your nose in other people's business
and putting your heart in other people's problems.

******

Saints are sinners who keep on trying.

Robert Louis Stevenson

Chapter 5   Habit

The Fence

There was a little boy with a bad temper. His father gave him a bag of nails and told him that every time he lost his temper, to hammer a nail in the back fence. The first day the boy had driven 37 nails into the fence. Then it gradually dwindled down. He discovered it was easier to hold his temper than to drive those nails into the fence.

Finally the day came when the boy didn't lose his temper at all. He told his father about it and the father suggested that the boy now pull out one nail for each day that he was able to hold his temper. The days passed and the young boy was finally able to tell his father that all the nails were gone.

The father took his son by the hand and led him to the fence. He said, "You have done well, my son, but look at the holes in the fence. The fence will never be the same. When you say things in anger, they leave a scar just like this one.

You can put a knife in a man and draw it out. It won't matter how many times you say I'm sorry, the wound is still there. A verbal wound is as bad as a physical one."

Author Unknown

Whoever covers over his sins does not prosper.

Whoever confesses and abandons them receives compassion.

Proverbs 28:13

******

Close your eyes to the faults of others and

you open the doors to friendship.

Chapter 5   Habit

You are a composite of the things you say, the books you read,
the thoughts you think, the company you keep,
and the things you desire to become.

******

If you were on trial for being a Christian,
would there be enough evidence to convict you?

******

God's way may be harder for you, but it will easier on you.

H. Hanson

******

Call to me and I will answer you.
I will tell you great and mysterious things that you did not know.

Jeremiah 33:3

******

If you can't find anything nice to say about your friends,
you have the wrong friends. Liking others is the key to being liked.

Chapter 5   Habit

The Station

Tucked away in our subconscious is an idyllic vision. We see ourselves on a long trip that spans the continent. We are traveling by train. Out the windows we drink in the passing scene of cars on nearby highways, of children waving at a crossing, of cattle grazing on a distant hillside, of smoke pouring from a power plant, of row upon row of corn and wheat, of flatlands and valleys, mountains and rolling hillsides, of city skylines and village halls.

But, uppermost in our minds is the final destination. Bands will be playing and flags waving, Once we get there our dreams will come true, and the pieces of our lives will fit together like a jigsaw puzzle. How restlessly we pace the aisles, damning the minutes for loitering -- waiting, waiting for the station.

"When we reach the station, that will be it," we cry.

"When I'm 18."

"When I buy a new Mercedes-Benz!"

"When I put the last child through college."

"When I have paid off the mortgage."

"When I get a promotion."

"When I reach the age of retirement, I shall live happily ever after!"

Sooner or later, we must realize there is no station, no one place to arrive at once and for all. The true joy of life is the trip. The station is only a dream. It constantly outdistances us.

"Relish the moment" is a good motto, especially when coupled with Psalm 118:24: ***"This is the day which the Lord hath made; we will rejoice and be glad in it."*** It isn't the burdens of today that drive us mad. It is the regrets over yesterday and the fear of tomorrow. Regret and fear are twin thieves who rob us of today.

So, stop pacing the aisles and counting the miles. Instead, climb more mountains, eat more ice cream, go barefoot more often, swim more rivers, watch more sunsets. laugh more, cry less. Live life as you go along. The station will come soon enough.

Robert Hastings

Chapter 5   Habit

The Four D's

Defeat comes from looking back.

Discouragement comes from looking down.

Distraction comes from looking around.

Deliverance comes from looking up.

******

The best cure for shaking knees is to kneel on them.

******

The only competition worthy of a wise man is with himself.

Washington Allston

******

This above all; to thine own self be true, and it must follow,

as the night the day, thou cannnot be false to any man.

Shakespeare

When love and skill work together, expect a masterpiece.

John Ruskin

******

Regret for the things we did can be tempered by time;

it is regret for the things we did not do that is inconsolable.

Sydney J. Harris

Chapter 5   Habit

He has shown you, O man, what is good, And what

does the Lord require of you but to do justly,

to love mercy, and to walk humbly with your God.

Micah 6:8

******

Trust the Lord with all you heart, and do not rely

on your own understanding. In all your ways

acknowledge Him, and He will make your paths smooth.

Proverbs 3:5-6

******

What we have done for ourselves alone dies with us.

What we have done for others and the world remains immortal.

Albert Pine

Perseverance is the key ...... having perseverance means persevering through failure. I love to talk about my successes, but the only way that I've ever learned anything is through failure.

You have to live through failure to understand how to succeed. And those are the lessons you never forget.

Martin Cooper

Use what talents you possess; the woods would be very silent

if no birds sang there except those that sang best.

Henry Van Dyke

Chapter 5   Habit

Don't do anything twice that you don't want for a habit!

Two Days

There are two days in every week about which we should not worry, two days which should be kept free from fear and apprehension. One of these days is yesterday with all its mistakes and cares, its faults and blunders, its aches and pains.

Yesterday has passed forever beyond our control. All the money in the world cannot bring back yesterday. We cannot undo a single act we performed; we cannot erase a single word we said. Yesterday is gone forever.

The other day we should not worry about is tomorrow with all its possible adversities, its burdens, its large promise and its poor performance; Tomorrow is also beyond our immediate control. Tomorrow's sun will rise, either in splendor or behind a mask of clouds, but it will rise. Until it does, we have no stake in tomorrow, for it is yet to be born.

This leaves only one day, today. Any person can fight the battle of just one day. It is when you and I add the burdens of those two awful eternities, yesterday and tomorrow, that we break down. It is not the experience of today that drives a person mad, it is the remorse or bitterness of something which happened yesterday and the dread of what tomorrow may bring.

Let us, therefore, Live but one day at a time.

Author Unknown

Chapter 5   Habit

I expect to pass through the world but once. Any good therefore
that I can do, or any kindness I can show to any creature, let me
do it now. Let me not defer it, for I shall not pass this way again.

Stephen Grellet

******

Your date book is your creed.

What you believe in, you have time for.

******

The best thing to do behind a person's back is to pat it.

Do good to your friend to keep him, to your enemy to gain him.

******

Do not let any unwholesome talk come out of your mouths,

only what is helpful for building others up.

Ephesians 4:29

******

Beware of the barrenness of a busy life.

Socrates

Blessed are they that have the gift of making

friends, for it is one of God's best gifts.

It involves many things, but above all, the power of

going out of one's self, and appreciating whatever

is noble and loving in another.

Thomas Hughes

97

Chapter 5   Habit

Envy is a symptom of lack of appreciation of our own
uniqueness and self worth.   Each of us has something
to give that no one else has.

Elizabeth O'Connor

******

He that is slow to anger is better than the mighty;
and he who rules his spirit than he who takes a city.

Proverbs 16:32

******

The important thing in this world is not
where we stand, but in what direction we move.

Goethe

******

A person's steps are directed by the Lord,
and the Lord delights in his way.

Psalm 37:23

******

It isn't that load that weighs us down - it's the way we carry it.

******

You may look lightly upon the Scripture
and see nothing; meditate often upon it and there
you shall see a light like the light of the sun.

Joseph Carry

Chapter 5   Habit

> It's All In A State Of Mind
>
> If you think you are beaten, you are;
>
> If you think you dare not, you won't.
>
> If you like to win, but don't think you can,
>
> It's almost a cinch you won't.
>
> Life's battles don't always go
>
> To the stronger or faster man,
>
> But sooner or later, the man who wins
>
> Is the fellow who thinks he can.

More people fail through lack of purpose than lack of talent.

Billy Sunday

******

Worry does not empty tomorrow of its sorrow.

It empties today of its strength.

Corrrie Ten Boom

******

I am indeed rich since my income is superior

to my expenses and my expenses are equal to my wishes.

Edward Gibbon

Chapter 5　　　Habit

Persistence

Nothing in the world can take the place of persistence. Talent will not; nothing is more common than unsuccessful men with talent.

Genius will not; unrewarded genius is almost a proverb. Education will not: the world is full of educated derelicts.

Persistence and determination are alone supreme.

Calvin Coolidge

If you're too busy to pray, you're too busy.

******

Motivation is what gets you started, habit is what keeps you going.

******

Wait on the Lord: be of good courage, and he shall

strengthen your heart: wait, I say, on the Lord.

Psalm 27:14

******

We are never more discontented with others

than when we are discontented with ourselves.

There is no such thing as can't, only won't. If you're qualified, all it takes is a burning desire to accomplish, to make a change.

Go forward, go backward. Whatever it takes! But you can't blame other people or society in general. It all comes from your mind. When we do the impossible we realize we are special people.

Jan Ashford

If you want your children to keep their feet on the ground,
put responsibility on their shoulders.

******

Doing the right thing is easy.
Trying to figure out what that is, is difficult.

Harry S. Truman

******

Our decisions are worth nothing until we form habits
around those decisions to keep ourselves going.

******

By doing nothing, you are not passing time, time is passing you.

******

Train up a child in the way he should go
and when he is old he will not depart from it.

Proverbs 22:6

Chapter 5   Habit

Kindness consists in loving people more than they deserve.

Joseph Joubert

******

I can give you a six-word formula for success:

Think things through - - then follow through.

Eddie Rickenbacker

******

Well done is better than well said.

Benjamin Franklin

Four Lessons on Life

1. Never take down a fence until you know why it was put up.

2. If you get too far ahead of the army, your soldiers may mistake you for the enemy.

3. Don''t complain about the bottom rungs of the ladder; they helped to get you higher.

4. If you want to enjoy the rainbow, be prepared to endure the storm.

Warren Wiersbe

Chapter 5   Habit

It is one of the most beautiful compensations of this life
that no one can sincerely try to help another without helping himself.

Ralph Waldo Emerson

******

We are not permitted to choose the frame of our destiny.
But what we put into it is ours.

Dag Hammargskjold

******

Flatter me, and I may not believe you. Criticize me, and I
may not like you. Ignore me, and I may not forgive you.
Encourage me, and I may not forget you.

William Arthur

******

Just because things go wrong is no reason
you have to go with them.

******

It is equally as important to keep the promises we
make to ourselves, as it is to keep
the promises we make to others.

******

No man was ever honored for what he received.
Honor has been the reward for what he gave.

Calvin Coolidge

Chapter 5   Habit

If a child lives with honesty, he learns what truth is.

If a child lives with fairness, he learns what justice is.

If a child lives with encouragement, he learns self-confidence.

If a child lives with fear, he learns to be apprehensive.

If a child lives with criticism, he learns to condemn.

******

We cannot do everything at once, but we can do something at once.

Calvin Coolidge

The Bridge of Life

The long span of the bridge of life is supported by countless cables called habits, attitudes, and desires.

What you do in life depends on what you are and what you want. What you get from life depends upon how much you want it - how much you are willing to work and plan and cooperate and use your resources.

The long span of the bridge of your life is supported by countless cables that you are spinning now, and that is why today is such an important day.

Make the cable strong.

L.G. Elliot

Chapter 5   Habit

Don't allow anything in your life that
you don't want reproduced in your children's lives.

******

The heights by great men reached and kept were
not attended by sudden flight, but they, while their
companions slept, were toiling upward in the night.

Henry Wadsworth Longfellow

******

He who runs from God in the morning
will scarcely find him the rest of the day.

John Bunyan

Some "Rules" For Living

The **Golden Rule**   "Do unto others as you would have them do unto you"

The **Silver Rule**   "At least do for yourself what you would do for others"

The **Iron Rule**   "Don't do for others what they can do for themselves"

The biblical command to love your neighbor as yourself implies a balance between caring for others and caring for oneself. If you don't love yourself, you can't love your neighbor.

Pastor Ronald Weinelt

Chapter 5   Habit

Delay is the deadliest form of denial.

C. Northcote Parkinson

Anna Mary Robertson married Tom Moses and had ten children. When Anna Mary got older, she was plagued with arthritis in her hands. At the age of eighty, she was looking for a pastime and took up painting because she found the paintbrush easy to hold.

Today, we know her as Grandma Moses, who painted more than fifteen hundred paintings. Twenty-five percent of them (375) paintings were done after she was one hundred years old!

Chapter 6

Goals

The word, **Goal**, is defined as the end toward which effort is directed; the purpose toward which an endeavor is directed; an end or objective.   Synonyms for goal, include aim, target, objective,, destination, aspiration, dream, hope, end, or intent. The word, goal, comes from the Middle English *gol:* boundary, or limit.

We must understand, as we are establishing our goals, that the true measures of success are seeking God's heart and obeying God's will. God will have His way, whether or not we go along with His ideas. Our challenge is to make and possess goals that are in alignment with God's intentions and desires for us.

Often, however, we are like Alice in *"Alice in Wonderland"*, when she came to a junction in the road leading in two different directions.

She asked the Cheshire Cat, "...would you tell me please, which way I ought to go from here?" "That depends on where you want to go," said the Cat.

"I don't much care where," replied Alice. "Then, it doesn't matter which way you go," replied the Cat.

Trust in the Lord with all your heart, and lean not

on your own understanding. In all your ways

acknowledge Him, and He shall direct your paths.

Proverbs 3:5-6

Chapter 6   Goals

Commit your works to the Lord,
and your thoughts will be established.
Proverbs 16:3
******

Far away in the sunshine are my highest aspirations.

I may not reach them, but I can look up and see their beauty,

believe in them, and try to follow where they lead.

Louisa May Alcott

The Road To Success Is Not Straight:

There is a curve called failure ...

A loop called confusion ...

Speed bumps called friends ...

Red lights called enemies...

Caution lights called family ...

You will have flats called jobs ...

. BUT..

If you have a spare called determination ....

An engine called perseverance...

Insurance called faith...

A driver called Jesus

You will make it to a place called success

Chapter 6   Goals

Great men are those who find that what they ought to do
and what they want to do are the same thing.

******

I know the plans that I have for you, declares the Lord.
They are plans for peace and not disaster,
plans to give you a future filled with hope.

Jeremiah 29:11

******

He who seeks applause from without has
all his happiness in another's keeping.

******

If you can believe, all things are
possible to him who believes.

Mark 9:23b

******

Nothing will ever be attempted if all
possible objections must be first overcome.

Samuel Johnson

Chapter 6   Goals

Put yourself in the other fellow's shoes

and you will never step on his toes

The Chicken

Once upon a time, there was a large mountainside, where an eagle's nest rested. The eagle's nest contained four large eagle eggs. One day an earthquake rocked the mountain causing one of the eggs to roll down the mountain, to a chicken farm, located in the valley below. The chickens knew that they must protect and care for the eagle's egg, so an old hen volunteered to nurture and raise the large egg.

One day, the egg hatched and a beautiful eagle was born. Sadly, however, the eagle was raised to be a chicken. Soon, the eagle believed he was nothing more than a chicken. The eagle loved his home and family, but his spirit cried out for more. While playing a game on the farm one day, the eagle looked to the skies above and noticed a group of mighty eagles soaring in the skies. "Oh," the eagle cried, "I wish I could soar like those birds." The chickens roared with laughter, "You cannot soar with those birds. You are a chicken and chickens do not soar."

The eagle continued staring, at his real family up above, dreaming that he could be with them. Each time the eagle would let his dreams be known, he was told it couldn't be done. That is what the eagle learned to believe. The eagle, after time, stopped dreaming and continued to live his life like a chicken. Finally, after a long life as a chicken, the eagle passed away.

The moral of the story: You become what you believe you are; so if you ever dream to become an eagle follow your dreams, not the words of a chicken.

Gary Barnes

Chapter 6   Goals

Grow Great By Dreams

The question was once asked of a highly successful businessman: "How have you done so much in your lifetime?"

He replied, "I have dreamed. I have turned my mind loose to imagine what I wanted to do. Then I have gone to bed and thought about my dreams. In the night I dreamt about my dreams. And when I awoke in the morning, I saw the way to make my dreams real.

While other people were saying, 'You can't do that, it isn't possible,' I was well on my way to achieving what I wanted." As Woodrow Wilson, 28th President of the U.S., said: "We grow great by dreams. All big men are dreamers."

They see things in the soft haze of a spring day, or in the red fire on a long winter's evening. Some of us let these great dreams die, but others nourish and protect them; nourish them through bad days until they bring them to the sunshine and light which comes always to those who sincerely hope that their dreams will come true."

So please, don't let anyone steal your dreams, or try to tell you they are too impossible. Sing your song, dream your dreams, hope your hope and pray your prayer.

Unknown

Life isn't a little bundle of big things:

it's a big bundle of little things.

******

If you are wearing out the seat of your pants before you do your shoe soles, you're making too many contacts in the wrong place.

Chapter 6   Goals

The Lord says, I will instruct you.

I will teach you the way that you should go.

I will advise you as my eyes watch over you.

Psalm 32:8

The Winner

If you think you are beaten, you are; if you think you dare not, you don't;

If you'd like to win, but you think you can't, it's almost a cinch you won't.

If you think you'll lose, you've lost, for out in the world you find success begins with a fellow's will - it's all in the state of the mind.

If you think you're outclassed you are; you've got to think high to rise; you've got to be sure of yourself before you can ever win the prize.

Many a race is lost before ever a step is run; and many a coward fails before ever his work's begun.

Think big and your deeds will grow; think small and you'll fall behind: think that you can and you will.. it's all in the state of mind.

Life's battles don't always go to the stronger or faster man; but sooner or later the man who wins is the fellow who thinks he can.

-- Author Unknown –

Chapter 6   Goals

If you limit your choices only to what
seems possible or reasonable,
you disconnect yourself from what you
truly want and all that is left is a compromise.

Robert Fritz

******

Always bear in mind that our own resolution to succeed
is more important than any other one thing.

Abraham Lincoln

The Power of Little Things

It takes a little muscle, and it takes a little grit,

A little true ambition, with a little bit of wit;

It's not the biggest things that count and make the biggest show;

It's the little things that people do that makes this old world go.

A little bit of smiling, and a little sunny chat,

A little bit of courage, to a comrade slipping back;

It takes a kindly action, and it takes a word of cheer,

To fill a life with sunshine, and to drive away a tear;

Great things are not the biggest things that make the biggest show;

It's the little things that people do, that make this old world go.

Anonymous

Chapter 6   Goals

You've got to be very careful if you don't know
where you are going, because you might not get there.

Yogi Berra

******

A note on the church bulletin board said:
"Good intentions, like crying babies, should be
carried out immediately. "

******

*Love the Lord your God with all your heart,
with all your soul, and with all your strength.*

Deuteronomy 6:5

******

If you have accomplished all that you planned
for your life, you have not planned enough!

******

Give me a stock clerk with a goal,
and I will give you a man who will make history.
Give me a man without a goal, and I will give you a stock clerk.

J. C. Penney

******

Entrust your efforts to the Lord, and your plans will succeed.

Proverbs 16:3

Chapter 6   Goals

Six Ways To Bury A Good Idea

1.   It will never work.

2.   We can't afford it.

3.   We've never done it that way before.

4.   We're not ready for it.

5.   It's not our responsibility.

6.   We're doing fine without it.

We all have good intentions we never follow through on.

Losing weight, getting more exercise...... Someday....

Unfortunately, _someday_ isn't a day on the calendar.

******

You do not have because you do not ask.

You ask and do not receive, because you ask amiss,

that you may spend it on you own pleasures..

James 4:2b-3

******

You'll never plough a field by turning it over in your mind.
Irish Proverb

Chapter 6   Goals

God's gifts put man's best dreams to shame.
Elizabeth Barrett Browning

There is a story about a bloodhound who, as he was chasing a deer, saw a fox crossing his path. So, he started chasing the fox instead. After a while, a rabbit crossed his path, so the hound chased the rabbit. Yet later, a mouse crossed his path and the hound chased the mouse into a hole. The hound, which had begun his hunt on the trail of a magnificent deer, ended up watching a mouse hole!

Aren't we, like the hound, all too often distracted and sidetracked? It is so easy to start well but then run after things that cross our paths, so that we end up chasing the wrong things.

It is not the words of our enemies that defeat us,
rather it is the silence of our friends.
Martin Luther King, Jr.
******

*I have fought the good fight, I have finished
the race, I have kept the faith.*
2nd Timothy 4:7
******

Well done is better than well said.
New England Proverb
******

The smallest good deed is better than the grandest good intention.
Duguet
******

*Trust the Lord with all your heart, and do not rely
on your own understanding. In all your ways
acknowledge Him, and He will make your paths smooth.*
Proverbs 3:5-6

Chapter 6   Goals

Goals are dreams with deadlines.
Diana Scharf Hunt
******

It is better to know some of the questions than all of the answers.
James Thurber
******

The minute you start talking about what you are
going to do if you lose, you have lost.
George P. Shultz
******

You will never "find" time for anything.
If you want time you must make it.
Charles Buxton
******

Anyone can carry his burden, however, hard, until nightfall.
Any one can do his work, however hard, for one day.
Any one can live sweetly, lovingly, purely, till the sun goes down.
And this is all that life really means.
Robert Louis Stevenson
******

Finish each day and be done with it ...
You have done what you could;
some blunders and absurdities no doubt crept in;
forget them as soon as you can.
Tomorrow is a new day; you shall begin it well and serenely.
Ralph Waldo Emerson
******

A long life may not be good enough, but a good life is long enough.
Benjamin Franklin

Chapter 6   Goals

A Creed to Live By

Don't undermine your worth by comparing yourself with others.

It is because we are different that each of us is special.

Don't set your goals by what other people do.

Only you know what is best for you.

Don't take for granted the things closest to your heart.

Cling to them as you would your life, for without them life is meaningless.

Don't let your life slip through your fingers by living in the past or for the future. By living your life one day at a time, you live all the days of your life.

Don't give up when you still have something to give.

Nothing is really over until the moment you stop trying.

Don't be afraid to admit that you are less than perfect.

It is this fragile thread that binds us to each other.

Don't be afraid to encounter risks.

It is by taking chances that we learn how to be brave.

Don't shut love out of your life by saying it's impossible to find.

The quickest way to receive love is to give love. The fastest way to lose love is to hold it too tightly; and the best way to keep love is to give it wings.

Don't dismiss your dreams.

To be without dreams is to be without hope; to be without hope is to be without purpose.

Don't run through life so fast that you forget not only where you've been, but also where you're going. Life is not a race, but a journey to be savored each step of the way.

Nancye Sims

Chapter 6   Goals

Preparation precedes performance.

There is no finer sensation in life than that which comes with victory over one's self. It feels good to go fronting into a hard wind, winning against its power; but it feels a thousand times better to go forward to a goal of inward achievement, brushing aside all your old internal enemies as you advance.

Vash Young

Perseverance is a great element of success. If you
only knock long enough and loud enough at the gate,
you are sure to wake up somebody.
Henry Wadsworth Longfellow

If you observe a really happy man you will find him building a boat, writing a symphony, educating his son, growing double dahlias in his garden, or looking for dinosaur eggs in the Gobi desert.

He will not be striving for it as a goal itself. He will have become aware that he is happy in the course of living life twenty-four crowded hours of the day.

W. Beran Wolfe

The greatest use of a life is to spend it
on something that will outlast it.
William James

Chapter 6   Goals

Your vision will be clear only when you look into your heart.
Who looks inside, dreams. Who looks inside awakens.
Carl Gustav Jung
******

The man who tries to do something and fails is infinitely
better off than he who tries to do nothing and succeeds.
Lloyd Jones
******

It is not because things are difficult that we do not dare;
it is because we do not dare that things are difficult.
Seneca

The Journey

If you don't keep walking you will never get where you're going.
Don't wait for someone to stop and carry you, you may weigh them down
and you both could fall.

When you think the walk is too steep, press on, for there is no
mountain that can't be climbed.

When you see someone fall along the way, lend your hand. If
someone lends you a hand, reach for it, to help you get back up again.

Hand in hand, together- each one helping the other can make this
journey as precious as the place that we are all striving for.

Author Unknown

---

*In everything give thanks, for this is the will
of God in Christ Jesus for you.*
1 Thessalonians 5:18

Chapter 6   Goals

So many of our dreams at first seem impossible,
then they seem improbable, and then, when we
summon the will, they soon become inevitable.
Christopher Reeve
******

Life offers two great gifts: time, and the ability to choose how we spend
it. Planning is a process of choosing among those many options. If we do
not choose to plan, then we choose to have others plan for us.
Richard I. Winword
******

My great concern is not whether you have failed,
but whether you are content with your failure.
Abraham Lincoln
******

You cannot depend on your eyes when
your imagination is out of focus.
Mark Twain
******

Do not go where the path may lead, go instead
where there is no path and leave a trail.
Ralph Waldo Emerson

An old pastor in Georgia used to make this statement: "When a
farmer prays for a corn crop, God expects him to say 'Amen' with a hoe."
If you are praying about a certain matter, get busy with it and pray. Be on
the job.

J. Vernon McGee

Perseverence is not a long race:
it is many short races one after another.
Walter Elliott

Chapter 7

Faith

The word, **Faith**, means a belief that does not rest on logical proof or material evidence; belief, trust, and loyalty to God; complete trust; something that is believed especially with strong conviction; a confident belief in the truth, value, or trustworthiness of a person, idea, or thing.

Synonyms for faith include: belief, hope, trust, certainty, expectation, reliance, conviction, and confidence. The word, faith, comes from the Middle English: *feith,* from Old French *feid, foi,* from Latin: *fides;* akin to Latin *fidere,* to trust.

God does not tell us to be successful, but faithful. Faith occurs when we cease trying to do something by our own efforts, and trust that God will do it for us. We declare, through our actions and responses to life's hazards, the degree to which we trust that God is truly in control. When we trust God, and respond in godly faith to life situations, events do not seem so overwhelming.

Faith grows from hearing. In Romans 10:17, we find: *So then faith comes by hearing, and hearing by the word of God.* On the path of faith we can expect to find sorrow and joy, suffering and healing, comfort, tears and smiles, trials and victories, conflicts and triumphs, and also hardships, dangers, beatings, persecutions, misunderstanding, trouble, and distress. *Yet 'in all these things we are more than conquerors through Him who loved us.* (Rom. 8:37).

So, we ought to keep on declaring the message He has given us. We can do no more. And, certainly, we cannot afford to do less!

Chapter 7   Faith

All scripture is given by inspiration of God, and is
profitable for doctrine, for reproof, for correction,
for instruction in righteousness, that the man of God
may be complete, thoroughly equipped for every good work.
2nd Timothy 3:16-17
******

But those who wait on the Lord shall renew their strength;
they shall mount up with wings like eagles,
they shall run and not be weary, they shall walk and not faint
Isaiah 40:31
******

Are You A Pumpkin?

A lady who had recently been saved was asked by one of her coworkers what it was like to be a Christian. She was caught off guard and didn't know how to answer, but when she looked up she saw a jack-o'-lantern on the desk and answered: "It's like being a pumpkin."

The worker asked her to explain that one. "Well, God picks you from the patch and brings you in and washes off all the dirt on the outside that you got from being around all the other pumpkins. Then He cuts off the top and takes all the yucky stuff out from inside. He removes all those seeds of doubt, hate, greed, etc. Then He carves you a new smiling face and puts His light inside of you to shine for all to see.

It is our choice to either stay outside and rot on the vine or come inside and be something new and bright."

I'll never look at a pumpkin the same way again.

For by grace you have been saved through faith; and that not of
yourselves: it is the gift of God; not of works, lest anyone should boast.
Ephesians 2:8-9

Chapter 7   Faith

For God so loved the world that He gave his only
begotten Son, that whoever believes in Him
should not perish, but have everlasting life.
John 3:16
******

Faith is the ability to trust God even when we do not understand
what He is doing. He knows and this is enough.
******

I do not want merely to possess a faith;
I want a faith that possesses me.
******

Now faith is the substance of things hoped for,
the evidence of things not seen.
Hebrews 11:1
******

We can only appreciate the miracle of sunrise
if we have waited in the darkness.
******

So then faith comes by hearing, and hearing by the word of God.
Romans 10:17
******

We should give as we would receive, cheerfully, quickly, and without
hesitation; for there is no grace in a benefit that sticks to the fingers.
Seneca
******

Little faith will bring your souls to Heaven,
but great faith will bring Heaven to your souls.
Charles H. Sturgeon

Chapter 7   Faith

What The Bible Means - A Child's Version

A father was approached by his small son, who told him proudly, "I know what the Bible means!"

His father smiled and replied, "What do you mean, you 'know" what the Bible means?" The son replied, "I do know!"

"Okay," said his father. "So, Son, what does the Bible mean?" "That's easy, Daddy. It stands for "Basic Instructions Before Leaving Earth."

We are hard-pressed on every side, yet not crushed;
we are perplexed, but not in despair;
persecuted, but not forsaken; struck down, but not destroyed
2nd Corinthians 4:8-9
******

The shortest distance between a problem and a solution
is the distance between your knees and the floor.
The one who kneels to the Lord can stand up to anything.
******

When you get to the end of all the light you know
and its time to enter into the darkness of the unknown,
faith is knowing that one of two things shall happen:
either you will be given something solid
to stand on, or you will be taught to fly.
Edward Teller
******

Don't be too anxious to give your children what you didn't have,
as you might neglect to give them what you did have.

Chapter 7   Faith

And this is the testimony: that God has given us eternal life,
and this life is in his Son. He that has the Son has life;
and he who does not have the Son of God does not have life.
1 John 5:11-12
******

When the child of God Looks into the Word of God
And sees the Son of God, He is changed by
the Spirit of God , For the Glory of God.
Warren Wiersbe
******

A faith that hasn't been tested can't be trusted.
Adrian Rogers
******

When one door closes, another opens, but we often
look so long and so regretfully upon the closed door
that we do not see the one that has opened for us.
Alexander Graham Bell
******

In the last analysis, our only freedom is
the freedom to discipline ourselves.
Bernard Baruch
******

Wait on the LORD; Be of good courage,
And He shall strengthen your heart; Wait, I say, on the LORD!
Psalm 27:14
******

It is impossible for that man to despair who
remembers that his Helper is omnipotent.
Jeremy Taylor

Chapter 7   Faith

The Biggest Mathematical Miracle In The World

Moses and his people were in the desert, but what was he going to do with them? They had to be fed, and fed is what he did, according to the Quartermaster General in the Army. It is reported that Moses would have to have had 1500 tons of food each day. Do you know that to bring that much food each day, two freight trains, each a mile long, would be required!

Besides you must remember, they were out in the desert, so they would have to have firewood to cook the food. This would take 4000 tons of wood and a few more freight trains, each a mile long, just for one day. And just think, they were forty years in transit. And oh yes! They would have to have water. If they only had enough to drink and wash a few dishes, it would take 11,000,000 gallons each day, and a freight train with tank cars, 1800 miles long, just to bring water!

And then another thing! They had to get across the Red Sea at night. (They did?) Now, if they went on a narrow path, double file, the line would be 800 miles long and would require 35 days and nights to get through. So, there had to be a space in the Red Sea, 3 miles wide so that they could walk 5000 abreast to get over in one night.

But then, there is another problem. Each time they camped at the end of the day, a campground two-thirds the size of the state of Rhode Island was required, or a total of 750 square miles long...think of it! This space just for nightly camping. Do you think Moses figured all this out before he left Egypt? I think not! You see, Moses believed in God. God took care of these things for him.

Now do you think God has any problem taking care of all your needs?

Chapter 7   Faith

In Christianity, there are three R's:
Relax in God's peace
Refresh in God's energies,
Relinquish to God's wisdom and will.
******

This is a faithful saying: For if we died
with Him, We shall also live with Him.
2 Timothy 2:11
******

But He knows the way that I take;
when He has tested me, I will come forth as gold.
Job 23:10
******\

When we rely upon education, we get what education can do.
When we rely on eloquence, we get what eloquence can do.
But when we rely on the Holy Spirit, we get what God can do.
A.C. Dixon
******

Faith is the daring of the soul to go farther than it can see.
William Newton Clark
******

Jesus said, "I am the light of the world. He who follows
me shall not walk in darkness, but will have the light of life."
John 8:12a
******

Faith came singing into my room and other guests took flight.
Grief, anxiety, fear and gloom, sped out into the night.
Elizabeth Cheney

Chapter 7   Faith

If your troubles aren't big enough to pray about,
then they certainly aren't big enough to worry and fret about.

He who is faithful in what is least is faithful also in much;
and he who is unjust in what is least is unjust also in much.
Luke 16:10

You're In Good Company

There are many reasons why God shouldn't have called you. But don't worry. You're in good company:

Moses stuttered	David's armor didn't fit.
John Mark was rejected by Paul	Timothy had ulcers.
Hosea's wife was a prostitute	Amos' only training was in the school of fig-tree pruning.
Jacob was a liar	David had an affair.
Solomon was too rich	Jesus was too poor.
Abraham was too old	David was too young.
Peter was afraid of death	Lazarus was dead.
John was self-righteous	Naomi was a widow.
Paul was a murderer	So was Moses.
Jonah ran from God	Miriam was a gossip.
Gideon and Thomas both doubted	Jeremiah was depressed and suicidal.
Elijah was burned out	John the Baptist was a loudmouth.
Martha was a worrywart	Mary was lazy.
Samson had long hair	Noah got drunk.
Moses had a short fuse	So did Peter, Paul-well, lots of folks did.

Chapter 7   Faith

Faith is the inborn capacity to see God behind everything.
Oswald Chambers

PRAYER

May today there be peace within you. May you trust God that you are exactly where you are meant to be. May you not forget the infinite possibilities that are born of faith.

May you use those gifts that you have received, and pass on the love that has been given to you. May you be content knowing that you are a child of God.

Let His presence settle into your bones, and allow your soul the freedom to sing, dance, and to bask in the sun. It is there for each and every one of you.

Thankfulness is the soil in which joy thrives.
******
In prayer it is better to have a heart
without words than words without heart.
John Bunyan
******
There are two worlds: the world that we can measure
with line and rule, and the world that we feel
with our hearts and imagination.
Leigh Hunt

Chapter 7   Faith

Faith Can Move Mountains

A small congregation in the foothills of the Great Smokies built a new sanctuary on a piece of land willed to them by a church member. Ten days before the new church was to open, the local building inspector informed the pastor that the parking lot was inadequate for the size of the building. Until the church doubled the size of the parking lot, they would not be able to use the new sanctuary.

Unfortunately, the church with its undersized lot had used every inch of their land except for the mountain against which it had been built. In order to build more parking spaces, they would have to move the mountain out of the back yard. Undaunted, the pastor announced the next Sunday morning that he would meet that evening with all members who had "mountain moving faith." They would hold a prayer session asking God to remove the mountain from the back yard and to somehow provide enough money to have it paved and painted before the scheduled opening dedication service the following week.

At the appointed time, 24 of the congregation's 300 members assembled for prayer. They prayed for nearly three hours. At ten o'clock the pastor said the final "Amen." "We'll open next Sunday as scheduled," he assured everyone. "God has never let us down before, and I believe He will be faithful this time too."

The next morning as he was working in his study there came a loud knock at his door. When he called "come in," a rough looking construction foreman appeared, removing his hard hat as he entered. "Excuse me, Reverend. I'm from Acme Construction Company over in the next county. We're building a huge new shopping mall over there and we need some fill dirt. Would you be willing to sell us a chunk of that mountain behind the church? We'll pay you for the dirt we remove and pave all the exposed area free of charge, if we can have it right away. We can't do anything else until we get the dirt in and allow it to settle properly."

The little church was dedicated the next Sunday as originally planned and there were far more members with "mountain moving faith" on opening Sunday than there had been the previous week!

Would you have shown up for that prayer meeting? Some people say faith comes from miracles. But others know: MIRACLES COME FROM FAITH!

Chapter 7   Faith

Worry is a thin stream of fear trickling through
the mind. If encouraged, it cuts a channel into
which all other thoughts are drained.
A.S. Roch
******

Man has not invented God; he has
developed faith, to meet a God already there.
Edna St. Vincent Millay
******

God the Father loves you; He sent His son.
God the Son loves you: He died for you.
And God the Holy Spirit loves you,
for He is now at your heart's door knocking.
J. Vernon McGee

Skeptic David Hume was seen walking in the snow long before daybreak one frigid morning. He, along with many others, was making his way to a little chapel where the famous preacher, George Whitefield was preaching

Someone who knew the skeptic said to him, "Mr. Hume, I didn't know you believed this message!" He responded, "I don't, but that man in the chapel does, and I can't stay away."

Don't let others spoil your faith and joy with
their philosophies, their wrong and shallow answers
built on men's thoughts and ideas, instead of what Christ has said.
Colossians 2:8

Chapter 7   Faith

Edwin M. Kerlin told of a minister who tried to comfort a woman who had endured great trouble.   Nothing he said seemed to cheer her or restore her faith.

He picked up some embroidery work she had laid aside and said, "What a confusion of threads!   Why waste time on a thing like that?" Turning the embroidery over, the woman said, "Now look at it.   You were seeing it from the wrong side."

"That's exactly right," replied the minister.   "And you are looking at your trials from the wrong side.   Turn them over and look at them from the right side - God's side.   The Lord is working out a design of His own for your life.   You must look at things from His point of view, and trust His workmanship."

Like Job and his friends, we often look in the wrong place to find reasons for trials.   Pray for faith to trust God when you cannot understand.

Does the place you're called to labor seem so small and little known?
It is great if God is in it, and He'll not forget His own.
Suffield
******

Now this is the confidence which we have in Him,
that if we ask anything according to His will, He hears us.
1 John 5:14

John Newton said, "If I ever reach heaven I expect to find three wonders there: first, to meet some I had not thought to see there; second, to miss some I had expected to see there; and third, the greatest wonder of all, to find myself there."

True faith obeys without delay.

Chapter 7   Faith

A faith worth having is a faith worth sharing.
.******

*Even though I walk through the valley of the
shadow of death, I will fear no evil, for you are with me.*
Psalm 23:4
******

Hope itself is like a star - not to be seen in the sunshine
of prosperity, and only to be discovered in the night of adversity.
Charles H. Spurgeon

Donald Barnhouse was the pastor of Philadelphia's Tenth Presbyterian Church when his wife died and left him with young daughters to raise alone. He conducted his own wife's funeral. While driving to that funeral, he realized that he had to say something to his girls to somehow put in perspective for them something with which he himself was already struggling.

They stopped at a traffic light. It was a bright day, and the sun was streaming into the car. A truck pulled up next to them and its shadow darkened the inside of the car. Barnhouse turned to his daughters and asked, "Would you rather be hit by the shadow or by the truck?"

One of them responded, "Oh, Daddy, that's a silly question! The shadow can't hurt you. I'd rather be hit by a shadow than by a truck."

Then he explained that their mother had died and that it was as if she'd been hit by a shadow. It was as if Jesus had stepped in the way in her place, and it was He who'd been hit by the truck. He then quoted the familiar words of Psalm 23:4.

Keith Anderson

Chapter 7   Faith

I do not pray for success, I ask for faithfulness.

Mother Teresa

If, as Herod, we fill our lives with things, and again with things; if we consider ourselves so unimportant that we must fill every moment our lives with action, when will we have the time to make the long, slow journey across the desert as did the Magi?

Or sit and watch the stars as did the shepherds? Or brood over the coming of the child as did Mary? For each one of us, there is a desert to travel. A star to discover. And a being within ourselves to bring to life.

Author Unknown

Be careful for nothing; but in every thing by prayer and supplication with thanksgiving let your requests be made known unto God

Philippians 4:6

Prayer: In Acceptance There Is Peace

Lord, I don't pray for tranquility, or that my problems

may cease; I pray that Your Spirit and Love would

give me strength to abide in You during adversity.

Amen

Chapter 7   Faith

Seek not so much to be understood as to understand.

St. Francis of Assisi

******

Yesterday is a canceled check, tomorrow is a promissory note;

Today is the only cash you have - so spend it wisely.

Kay Lyons

******

Come to Me, all you who labor and are

heavy laden, and I will give you rest.

Matthew 11:28

******

There are many things that are essential to arriving at

true peace of mind, and one of the most important is faith,

which cannot be acquired without prayer.

John Wooden

> Suppose a nation in some distant region should take a Bible for their only law book, and every member should regulate his conduct by the precepts there contained!
>
> Every member would be obliged in conscience to temperance, frugality and industry; to justice, kindness, and charity toward his fellow men; and to piety, love and reverence toward Almighty God..
>
> John Adams

Chapter 7   Faith

Use your gifts faithfully, and they shall be enlarged;

practice what you know, and you shall attain to higher knowledge.

Matthew Arnold

******

Your faith is what you believe, not what you know.

John Lancaster Spalding

Seeing the crowds, Jesus went up on the mountain, and when he sat down his disciples came to him. And he opened his mouth and taught them, saying:

"Blessed are the poor in spirit, for theirs is the kingdom of heaven.

"Blessed are those who mourn, for they shall be comforted.

"Blessed are the meek, for they shall inherit the earth.

"Blessed are those who hunger and thirst for righteousness, for they shall be satisfied.

"Blessed are the merciful, for they shall obtain mercy.

"Blessed are the pure in heart, for they shall see God.

"Blessed are the peacemakers, for they shall be called sons of God.

"Blessed are those who are persecuted for righteousness' sake, for theirs is the kingdom of heaven."

Matthew 5:1-10

Chapter 7   Faith

Every tomorrow has two handles. We can take hold of it
by the handle of anxiety, or by the handle of faith.

Unknown

******

I know that the Lord is always on the side of right.
But it is my constant anxiety and prayer that I,
and this nation, should be on the Lord's side.

Abraham Lincoln

If we were logical, the future would be bleak indeed. But we are
more than logical. We are human beings, and we have faith and we have
hope, and we can work.

Jacques Cousteau

Beloved, do not believe every spirit, but test the spirits,
whether they are of God , because many false prophets
are gone out into the world..... every spirit that confesses
that Jesus Christ has come in the flesh is of God.

1st John 4:1-2

******

Put God between yourself and the foe.
Believe that He is there between you and your difficulty,
and what baffles you will flee before Him, as clouds before the gale.

F.B. Meyer

138

Chapter 7   Faith

For I am not ashamed of the gospel of Christ:

for it is the power of God to salvation for everyone that believes...

Romans 1:16

On the night before his wedding, Joseph Scriven's fiancee drowned: devastated, Scriven moved away from his home to escape the memory of her.

He relocated to Canada where he met another lovely young women names Eliza. Before they could marry, she got sick and passed away.

Joseph Scriven, faced these and many other tragedies; however Christ was his constant comfort. It was Scriven who penned the beautiful poem, "What A Friend We Have In Jesus." He wrote, "Can we find a friend so faithful who will all our sorrows share? Jesus knows our every weakness; take it to the Lord in prayer."

When a man does not know what harbor

he is making for, no wind is the right wind.

Seneca

Chapter 7   Faith

For I am convinced that nothing can ever separate us
from his love. Death can't, and life can't The angels won't,
and all the power of hell itself cannot keep God's love away.

Romans 8:23

******

God has three answers to prayer: yes, no, and wait. He may say

yes or no immediately. Or He may say, "Wait until you

can properly use what you requested." If a request is not His

will, we should thank Him for not granting it.

(Pray that you will may be in harmony with His will.)

Herschel Hobbs

******

Faith is not belief without proof, but trust without reservation.

Elton Trueblood

******

If any man desires to come after Me,
let him deny himself, and take up his cross, and follow Me.

Matthew 16:24

******

Some men see things as they are and ask why.

Others dream things that never were and ask why not.

George Bernard Shaw

Chapter 7   Faith

Faith is the highest passion in a human being.

Many in every generation may not come that far,

but none comes further.

Soren Kerkegaard

******

For who shall separate us from the love of God? Shall tribulation, or distress, or persecution, or famine or nakedness, or peril, or sword?.... Yet in all things we are more than conquerors through Him who loved us. For I am persuaded that neither death or life, nor agents or principalities, nor powers, nor things present nor things to come, nor height nor depth, nor any other created things, shall be able to separate us from the love of God which is in Christ Jesus our Lord.

Romans 8:35, 37-39

******

If I take the wings of the morning and dwell

in the uttermost parts of the sea; Even there

Your hand shall lead me, and Your right hand shall hold me.

Psalm 139:9-10

******

To believe, and to consent to be loved

while unworthy, is the great secret.

W.R. Newell

******

Where the heart is willing, it will find a thousand ways,

but where it is unwilling, it will find a thousand excuses.

141

Chapter 7   Faith

Ron Dunn told the story about a time when his children were small and he took them to a carnival. He bought a long string of tickets, rolled them around his hand and passed them out to the kids whenever they discovered something they wanted to do. He said, "I stood right at the gate where the ticket taker was, and I gave out tickets to my kids, one at a time, as they went by.

There was a little towheaded boy who came by, and asked for a ticket. I said, ' I never saw you before.' The little fellow said, 'He said if I asked, you would give me a ticket.'

I looked over in the direction he looked and there was my son. At that moment, I would have given my whole roll of tickets to that kid for the sake of my son. In the same way, Christ is the heir of all things, For His sake you, too, can have all of the things He promised.

Faith is seeing a rainbow in each tear.

******

The Spirit itself bears witness with our spirit that we are children of God, and if children, then heirs- heirs of God and joint heirs with Christ, if indeed we suffer with Him, that we may also be glorified together.

Romans 8:15-17

******

Are your troubles causing you to
lose your religion or use your religion?

Chapter 7   Faith

God does not expect us to submit our faith to Him without reason,

but the very limits of our reason make faith a necessity.

Augustine

******

If my people, who are called by my name, will humble themselves, and
pray, and seek My face, and turn from their wicked ways; then I will
hear from heaven and will forgive their sin, and heal their land.

2nd Chronicles 7:14

******

Forgetting those things which are behind and reaching forward

to those things which are ahead, I press toward the goal

for the prize of the upward call of God in Christ Jesus..

Philippians 3:13a-14

Robert F. Litro, Ph.D., is a speaker, trainer, author, and consultant and founder of Dr. Bob Litro & Associates. Dr. Bob's insights have been developed from over thirty years experience as a public school teacher, college administrator, business professor, author, and consultant.

Dr. Litro holds B.S. and M.S. degrees from Central Connecticut State University and a Ph.D. degree from the University of Connecticut.

Bob lives in Jackson, MS, with his wife, Jane.